# One Man Stood Alone

July 15, 1936

*New York City*

It was another scorching-hot day in New York, but that didn't stop thousands of people from crowding the docks along the Hudson River. The scene looked and sounded like the Fourth of July. Bands played patriotic tunes as men, women, and children on both sides of the Hudson cheered and waved small American flags. At twelve noon, more than four hundred American athletes, coaches, officials, family members, and journalists would set sail on a nine-day journey aboard the SS *Manhattan* to Germany for the eleventh Olympic Games.

But pacing along the shore was a man who seemed out of place, different from the thousands who surrounded him. He walked silently, carrying a sign. It was an odd sign; the letters weren't all that neatly written. And its message was startling. BOYCOTT NAZI GERMANY, LAND OF DARKNESS. BOYCOTT HITLER. KEEP AMERICA FREE. FIGHT FOR RACE TOLERANCE, DEMOCRACY AND PEACE. I SPENT 10 MONTHS IN A NAZI JAIL FOR DEFENDING THESE PRINCIPLES.

Boycott? It was too late now. The SS *Manhattan* had left Pier 60 and was on its way toward the Statue of Liberty and the Atlantic Ocean. The people listening at home had turned off their radios. In seventeen days, the Olympics would begin with elaborate opening ceremonies broadcast from Berlin. The solitary protest of the courageous man with the sign, Richard Roiderer, would be long forgotten by then.

But maybe people should have paid closer attention. The man who stood alone understood there was more to this Olympics than met the eye. In Adolf Hitler's Berlin, all was not as it seemed.

## ALSO BY ANDREW MARANISS

*Strong Inside*

*Singled Out*


## OTHER BOOKS YOU MAY ENJOY

*The Boys in the Boat (Young Readers Adaptation)*
Daniel James Brown

*Legends: The Best Players, Games, and Teams in Basketball*
Howard Bryant

*Disaster Strikes!: The Most Dangerous Space Missions of All Time*
Jeffrey Kluger

*To the Moon!: The True Story of the American Heroes on the Apollo 8 Spaceship*
Jeffrey Kluger

# GAMES

## —OF—

# DECEPTION

### The True Story of the First
### U.S. Olympic Basketball Team at the
### 1936 Olympics in Hitler's Germany

## ANDREW MARANISS

PENGUIN BOOKS

Penguin Books
An imprint of Penguin Random House LLC, New York

First published in the United States of America by Philomel Books,
an imprint of Penguin Random House LLC, 2019
Published by Penguin Books, an imprint of Penguin Random House LLC, 2021

Philomel Books is a registered trademark of Penguin Random House LLC.

Visit us online at penguinrandomhouse.com.

LIBRARY OF CONGRESS CATALOGING-IN-PUBLICATION DATA IS AVAILABLE.

Printed in the United States of America.

Penguin Books ISBN 9780525514657

1 3 5 7 9 10 8 6 4 2

Edited by Jill Santopolo.
Design by Jennifer Chung.
Text set in Adobe Garamond.

*For Alison, Eliza, and Charlie,*

*my Dream Team*

# CONTENTS

# One Man Stood Alone

July 15, 1936

*New York City*

I t was another scorching-hot day in New York, but that didn't stop thousands of people from crowding the docks along the Hudson River.

The scene looked and sounded like the Fourth of July. Bands played patriotic tunes as men, women, and children on both sides of the Hudson cheered and waved small American flags. Even the SS *Manhattan* was dressed for the occasion, with its red hull, white superstructure, and red, white, and blue funnels. Planes circled overhead, and, out on the water, boats sounded their horns and shot streams of water high into the air in celebration.

As far away as Kansas and California, families gathered around their radios, listening to announcers describe the festivities. At twelve noon, more than four hundred American athletes, coaches, officials, family members, and journalists

*With members of the U.S. Olympic team aboard, the New York City skyline in the distance and thousands of fans cheering from the shore, the SS* Manhattan *sets off for Germany on July 15, 1936.* (New York Daily News)

would set sail on a nine-day journey to Germany for the greatest spectacle in the world, the eleventh Olympic Games.

But first, there was much to behold at Pier 60.

An African American man gave out homemade good-luck charms to the athletes as they boarded the ship, but he didn't even bother to hand one to the great black track star from Ohio State, Jesse Owens, telling onlookers that Owens wouldn't need any luck in Berlin.

Up on deck, a group of female athletes—there were a record number of them on this U.S. Olympic team—gathered in two rows for a photo. One woman called out, "We're going to bring home the bacon, aren't we, girls?!" and her teammates let out a big cheer.

And who was that sprinting up the gangplank onto the boat? It was Willard Schmidt, all six foot nine of him, a skinny Nebraska farm boy who was the last man added to the U.S. Olympic basketball team. He hurried on board so nobody could stop him. Just being on this ship and on this team felt like such an improbable dream he was afraid somebody would pinch him and it would all be over.

Next came Schmidt's USA Basketball teammates, including five more players from the Globe Refiners, his amateur team in McPherson, Kansas; seven from the Universals of Los Angeles; and one college player from the University of Washington. The Olympic team had been assembled by merging the two best amateur teams in the country (along with the one college player) after a qualifying tournament in New York where the Universals came in first and the Refiners second. The men who followed Schmidt onto the ship included Frank "Frankenstein" Lubin, a hulking six-foot-seven center; assistant coach Gene Johnson, stylishly dressed and talkative as usual; and his soft-spoken brother, Francis, a star of the team. Along, too, came Sam Balter from LA, and his buddies, Art Mollner, Carl Shy, and Carl Knowles. Lumbering aboard came big "College Joe" Fortenberry, the gentle giant from Happy, Texas. Tex Gibbons boarded the ship with one arm in a sling, while center Ralph Bishop from Washington, the only college player on the team, chatted with nine fellow UW Huskies, young men who would compete in a highly anticipated rowing event in Berlin. Rounding out the group were head coach Jimmy Needles, in desperate need of coffee (he drank twenty-five cups a day), along with Jack Ragland, Duane Swanson, Donald Piper, and Bill Wheatley.

The names of these men have been forgotten, but they were an important and historic group: 1936 marked basketball's debut as an official Olympic sport, and this was the first-ever United States Olympic basketball team. Decades later, the U.S. Olympic basketball team would be dubbed the Dream Team, and a new collection of superstars would command the world's attention at the Summer Olympics every four years. But for Oscar Robertson and Jerry West to win Olympic gold in 1960, for Michael Jordan, Magic Johnson, and Larry Bird to win in 1992, or for Kobe Bryant, LeBron James, and Kevin Durant to taste gold more recently, there had to be this bunch of no-names walking up the plank at Pier 60 in 1936.

As the SS *Manhattan* pushed back just past noon, fans tossed their caps into the air; some even threw them in the river. Bill Wheatley looked out at thousands of cheering New Yorkers and considered how far he'd come as a basketball player. He'd been cut from his college team. The coach told him he was no good. Now he was sailing to Europe to play the game he loved on the world's largest stage.

The ship pushed farther away, and the scene at the pier began to thin out, people clutching their flags and heading back home and to work.

But pacing along the shore was a man who seemed out of place, different from the thousands who surrounded him. He walked silently, carrying a sign. It was an odd sign; the letters weren't all that neatly written. And its message was startling. BOYCOTT NAZI GERMANY, LAND OF DARKNESS. BOYCOTT HITLER. KEEP AMERICA FREE. FIGHT FOR RACE TOLERANCE, DEMOCRACY AND PEACE. I SPENT 10 MONTHS IN A NAZI JAIL FOR DEFENDING THESE PRINCIPLES.

Boycott? It was too late now. The SS *Manhattan* had left Pier 60 and was on its way toward the Statue of Liberty and the Atlantic Ocean.

The people listening at home had turned off their radios. In seventeen days, the Olympics would begin with elaborate opening ceremonies broadcast from Berlin. The solitary protest of the courageous man with the sign, Richard Roiderer, would be long forgotten by then.

But maybe people should have paid closer attention. The man who stood alone understood there was more to this Olympics than met the eye. In Adolf Hitler's Berlin, all was not as it seemed.

# CHAPTER TWO

# A Sinister Façade

As the Americans on board the SS *Manhattan* watched the New York City skyline fade into the distance, four thousand miles ahead of them the finishing touches were applied to a city receiving an extreme makeover. Berlin had never looked better than it did in July 1936. It was as if the seven-hundred-year-old German capital had transformed into the world's largest movie set, a bright and shiny, picture-perfect fantasyland where every blade of grass was manicured, every smile permanently affixed and gleaming. A *New York Times* reporter called the massive undertaking a "civic clean-up unequaled in history."

There were big projects impossible to miss: dirt and grime washed away from centuries-old buildings, a subway line extending to the new 110,000-seat Olympic Stadium, fifty-foot banners lining downtown streets like a multicolored bamboo

*The streets of Berlin were clean and colorful in the summer of 1936. Visitors from around the world were impressed by the flowers, flags, and helpful guides. But the pretty scenes were all for show, obscuring an ugly truth about Hitler's Germany. Just up the road at Sachsenhausen, the Nazis were torturing political prisoners.* (U.S. Holocaust Memorial Museum, courtesy of National Archives and Records Administration)

forest, geraniums and fuchsias hanging from every windowsill along the main thoroughfares, and waltzes blaring from new outdoor speakers.

There were smaller touches, too. One American journalist noticed the carpet at his favorite neighborhood café had been replaced, as had the upholstery on the chairs. Vacant shops were suddenly alive with temporary new tenants. The air was filled with the smell of fresh paint.

The makeover applied to people, too. Nazi propaganda minister Joseph Goebbels, a small, clubfooted thirty-eight-year-old with slicked-back hair and enormous influence, issued a command to Berlin's citizens through *Der Angriff*, the Nazi newspaper he had founded. "We must be more charming than the Parisians, easier-going than the Viennese, livelier than the Romans, more cosmopolitan than Londoners, and more practical than New Yorkers."

Police officers exchanged their imposing military-style uniforms for a gentler look, complete with delicate white gloves. Maids, waiters, and waitresses at posh hotels like the Adler, Excelsior, and Eden learned handy English phrases so they could cheerfully communicate with guests. Tour guides on street corners wore miniature flags on their jacket lapels to indicate which languages they spoke. Even train conductors were hospitable. *Can I open your window to make you more comfortable, ma'am?*

But like a temporary movie set, this was all just a façade; it was for show, and it would disappear as soon as the Olympic guests went home. There was something sinister afoot. The flowers, the flags, the smiling faces—they weren't there to reveal the city's best self. They were meant to distract from terrible things happening behind the scenes.

Germany was now three years into the rule of dictator Adolf Hitler. His Nazi party had come to power in 1933 in the throes of the devastating global economic crisis known as the Great Depression, appealing to many Germans with calculated messages related to jobs, food, hatred of Jewish people, and rabid nationalism, which is not to be confused with patriotism. While patriotism can be defined as a healthy love for one's country, nationalists draw harsh distinctions between "us and them," implying the superiority of one group of people over all others. Truth and morality are cast aside in such a society; all that matters is advancing the cause of the favored group.

*Adolf Hitler is one of the most evil figures in the history of the world. His fascist, nationalist, and anti-Semitic regime ruled Germany from 1933–1945. In a state built on propaganda, the truth was the first casualty.* (U.S. Holocaust Memorial Museum, Unknown Provenance)

A vicious anti-Semitism, an illogical hatred of Jewish people that dated back centuries, was at the heart of Nazi doctrine. Though Jewish people made up less than one percent of the German population, the Nazis blamed Jewish people as the source of all the country's—and the world's—problems. In the autobiography he published before gaining power, *Mein Kampf*, Hitler called for the complete removal of Jewish people from Germany, and he was well on the way, already by 1936 having stripped Jewish people of political, economic, and legal rights— even of German citizenship. This was a classic fascist state—an oppressive, authoritarian government where political opposition of any kind was forbidden and individual liberty was an evil. People either served the interest of the Nazi state or were deemed disposable. Germans were told what to think and how to behave, and any deviations were subject to severe punishment.

On the eve of the 1936 Olympics, the Nazis weren't yet herding Jewish people into concentration camps in large numbers. The camps operated more like political prisons, meant to intimidate and silence opponents of Hitler's evil regime, no matter their religion. It was no coincidence the number of inmates in these prisons was rising as the world turned its attention to Germany for the Olympics. If the people who dared to speak out against Hitler were locked away, who could hear their protests?

Which is why for those who knew better, it was easy to see through the smoke screen of Berlin's happy transformation in the summer of 1936; they recognized it as just another manifestation of the Nazis' total control of German society. The jazz musicians the Nazis considered degenerate were again allowed in the cafés, and the same books Nazis had tossed into bonfires three years earlier were now restocked on the shelves of Berlin's bookstores, but none of this represented any change in the Nazis' philosophy and none of it would last beyond August. It was a coordinated effort—directed from the highest levels of government and carried out by the most ordinary citizens—meant to fool international Olympic visitors into believing the negative reports they'd heard about Hitler's Germany might not be accurate. For the Nazis, creating confusion about the truth was a victory.

*The Nazis were anti-intellectual cowards who opposed freedom of thought, freedom of speech, freedom of the press, and freedom of religion, to name a few. On May 10, 1933, they staged book burnings of texts they deemed threatening to their bigoted worldview.* (U.S. Holocaust Memorial Museum, courtesy of National Archives)

In a culture like this, one had to wonder if even the smiles were genuine. The Nazis declared a national "week of laughter" in mid-July, stating that "the coming eight days will be days of jollity and cheerfulness . . . None should miss this chance." In other words: be happy, or else!

Smiles in the daytime, tears in the darkness. In the middle of the night of July 16, police rousted Berlin's Romani citizens (sometimes derogatorily referred to as gypsies) from their sleep, herding six hundred men, women, and children off to a camp next to a sewage dump fifteen miles from the Olympic Stadium and out of sight of international visitors. For these families, this night of uncertainty and fear just ahead of the Olympics was the first step on a road of terror that would lead to their deaths in concentration camps. More than 1,400 homeless people were picked up off the streets, too, not to be fed or clothed, but to be imprisoned.

About twenty miles northwest of Berlin, near the town of Oranienburg, on the same day the U.S. Olympic team marched aboard the SS *Manhattan*, brutal Nazi guards forced political prisoners to clear a pine forest and begin constructing a new concentration camp known as Sachsenhausen. These prisoners weren't criminals as we understand the word in a free society. They hadn't hurt anyone or stolen anything. Rather, they were ordinary people who disagreed with the Nazis and were torn from their homes and families simply for their beliefs. They found themselves living a nightmare, kicked, whipped, tortured, beaten, and starved, one daily humiliation after another. The camp's medic was so twisted he became known as Dr. Gruesome.

By the end of 1936, more than 1,600 inmates suffered under these conditions at Sachsenhausen, and thousands more were on the way. As the world's attention turned toward Germany for the Olympics, Nazi brutality escalated rather than subsided. Total concentration camp populations doubled from 3,800 in the

*A prisoner at the Sachsenhausen concentration camp chops wood under forced labor conditions. While the Nazis would eventually use the concentration camp system to murder millions of Jewish people, initially they operated more as political prisons, locking away opponents of the Hitler regime under inhumane conditions.*
(U.S. Holocaust Memorial Museum, courtesy of National Archives)

summer of 1935 to 7,746 by the end of 1937. By 1938, it wasn't primarily political opponents who filled the camps, but Jewish people. And by the time Allied forces defeated the Nazis in World War II in 1945, Hitler's twelve-year reign of anti-Semitic violence had resulted in the murder of more than six million Jewish men, women, and children.

In the summer of 1936, when citizens of the world were mesmerized by an Olympic fantasy—the elaborate, colorful, and deceptive stage the Nazis built in Berlin—they would have been better served investigating the reality—dismal, dark, and violent—just up the road in Sachsenhausen. "The concentration camps," wrote one historian, "embodied the spirit of Nazism like no other institution."

Not everyone was fooled by the Nazis' big lie. In St. Louis, Missouri, Rabbi Ferdinand Isserman understood exactly what was happening. He warned his congregation not to be conned by the images coming out of Berlin, especially the reports of a beautiful, modern city and its citizens acting as one. Hitler's brand of harmony, he said, was nothing for Americans to admire.

"It is the unity enforced by cannon and not by conviction," he warned, "by fear and not by faith, by terror and not by truth."

Aboard the SS *Manhattan*, the U.S. basketball team was headed to one of the most barbaric places on the planet.

But the basketball players did not give this much thought. Instead, they were excited about sailing to Europe and the chance to win a gold medal, and they knew one very important figure would be there to see them play. It wasn't Adolf

Hitler, but a man who had dedicated his life to the principles of sportsmanship and fair play. The first Olympic basketball tournament would be the crowning achievement in the remarkable and quirky life of this seventy-four-year-old college professor, an orphaned former lumberjack from Almonte, Ontario.

He was the inventor of basketball, and his name was James Naismith.

# CHAPTER THREE

# Inventing a Game

December 20, 1891

*Springfield, Massachusetts*

Outside his bedroom window, snow fell silently in the night, another New England blizzard blanketing the landscape in white. Inside, by lamplight, James Naismith sat alone at his desk, forty-five years before the Berlin Olympics and just moments away from making history. Of course, Naismith didn't know that yet. Instead, he was frustrated. He hadn't solved the problem he'd worked on for two weeks, and time was running out. Either he figured it out before he fell asleep or he didn't; he'd be a success or a failure in the morning, and every passing second reminded him of this.

Naismith was thirty years old, a strong and sincere man—a devout one, too, intent on bringing young men closer to God through the ministry of athletics.

As a student in a new "Psychology of Play" course at the International YMCA

*James Naismith arrived at the International YMCA Training School in Springfield, Massachusetts, intent on using the power of sports to bring young men closer to God. He accepted a challenge to create a game that would keep students busy during the cold winter months—we call his invention basketball.*
(Springfield College Archives & Special Collections)

Training School in Springfield, where he studied and taught, Naismith had accepted a challenge from the director of the school's physical education program, Luther Gulick, to develop a new game, something to keep restless students occupied inside the gymnasium during the winter months. Two instructors had tried and failed at this assignment, run off by an unruly, hostile bunch of students who hated gymnastics, calisthenics, and marching in circles. Naismith made an offhand comment to Gulick that he could come up with a new game, and Gulick surprised him by replying, "Okay, fine, do it."

At first, Naismith tried to bring outdoor games inside. But football and lacrosse weren't well suited to the tiny gymnasium in the Armory Building. Too many injuries, too much broken equipment. Indoor soccer created the same problems. He tried safer diversions, kids' games like tag and leapfrog. But the students in this class were all in their twenties and thirties, older men on the way to managing YMCAs around the world. This wasn't elementary school recess.

Naismith regrouped. He knew he wanted a game that required an all-around athlete, one that was easy to learn but difficult to master, a team game, possible to play in any gymnasium. He wanted to eliminate rough play; a key breakthrough was the idea that a player could not run with the ball but must pass it to advance down the court (in the earliest days of basketball, there was no dribbling). He wanted a game that used a large, light ball, and not much other equipment. Slowly the contours of a new game began to form in his mind. The last problem to solve, the one that kept him up late, concerned how the players would score. Specifically, how the goal should be situated. And then, on this cold December night, his mind flashed back to his boyhood days in rural Ontario, Canada, to the blacksmith's shop in Bennie's Corners where he and his buddies congregated, watching the blacksmith at work while they played in the yard nearby. The boys called one of their favorite games Duck on a Rock. The object was to knock a stone off a much larger boulder. Kids would throw rocks at the stone sitting on the boulder, and if they failed, they'd have to scoop up their rock and return to base before they were tagged by the player designated as the guard. Over time, Naismith and his friends learned that a high-arching toss of their stone worked better than more of a straight baseball-style throw.

That was it! Naismith's new game required a toss with a high arc. The goal would be located high off the ground, parallel to the floor.

James Naismith put down his pencil and went to bed content on December 20, 1891. That night he became the first human being ever to play this new game, if only in his dreams.

# CHAPTER FOUR

# Do Good and Be Pure

James Naismith was the right person in the right place at the right time. If it hadn't been for the tragedies, accidents, hard work, good fortune, and unconventional decisions that led him to Springfield, there would be no game of basketball today. It's not as if the sport existed in the earth's crust, just waiting for someone to discover it. Instead, it sprang from the mind of a man whose life experiences all came together to create a new idea. Here's how it happened.

From age nine, Naismith grew up without his parents. It was his mother, Margaret, he missed most, a heavy sorrow he felt each day. When the pain overwhelmed him, he would run across the fields of his maternal grandmother's farm, slip into the barn, and climb into a grain bin where his mom had played as a child.

This is where he felt closest to her. He would sit in the bin and sob, and when the tears dried, he would speak, telling his mother about everything happening in his life. He knew she could hear him.

James remembered the last time he saw his mother, days before his ninth birthday in the late fall of 1870. She stood in the doorway, waving goodbye to her three children, Annie, James, and little Robbie, after shooing them out the door toward her brother William's horse-drawn sleigh. James's father was sick with typhoid fever, a deadly disease ravaging the town. Concerned for his niece and nephews, William told Margaret he was coming to pick up the kids while Margaret cared for her ailing husband. But John Naismith died, and then Margaret succumbed to the disease on November 6, the same day James turned nine and Annie turned twelve. Birthdays always remained a bittersweet occasion for James Naismith.

With his parents gone, Naismith and his siblings moved in with their grandmother. But she died two years later, and the kids were left in the hands of their uncle Peter, a bachelor and lumberjack in his midtwenties. Annie ran the home, which meant cooking, cleaning, and sewing. James walked three miles to school each morning, and when he wasn't studying, he was in the fields and forests, chopping down trees, sawing logs, and driving teams of horses. At age fifteen, he dropped out of school and went to work full time, drawn to the physical exertion, the outdoor life, and the paydays. There was no coddling from Uncle Peter or the lumberjacks. And if he tried to fit in with the older guys, that meant more than just wearing heavy boots. It meant foul language and drinking. Both in large quantities.

One day, James was downing whiskey at a local tavern when a man asked him if he was the son of Margaret Young. Yes, he said, drink in hand. "She'd turn over in her grave to see ye," the stranger replied.

The encounter was life-changing for young Naismith. He left the bar and walked home, heading straight for the grain bin, where he made a promise to his mother: she'd never be ashamed of him again.

At age twenty, he returned to high school, earning his diploma in just two years. Then it was on to McGill University in Montreal, where Uncle Peter paid James's tuition in exchange for summer work on the farm. At first, James was so intent on focusing on his academics that he refused to become involved in extra-curricular activities. But then two classmates showed up at his dorm room and urged him to join them in the gymnasium.

McGill was one of the first universities in North America to offer a physical education program, and the allure of athletics was too strong for Naismith to resist. He didn't just show up at the gym, he excelled in everything he tried—football, lacrosse, soccer, wrestling, and rugby—earning awards for his athletic achievements. When he graduated in 1887 and enrolled at nearby Presbyterian College to earn his master's in divinity, Naismith remained a fixture on the McGill campus, even running the gymnasium when the director died. As a student at Presbyterian, Naismith occasionally preached on Sundays. One morning he stood at the pulpit and delivered a sermon with two black eyes earned in a rough-and-tumble football game. Naismith was living a bold and unconventional life. Many in the church considered athletics to be the devil's work, pulling young men away from more worthwhile pursuits. Critics called lacrosse "legal-ized murder." But James saw opportunity where others did not. "I felt that if the devil was making use of athletics to lead young men to evil," he said, "there must be some natural attraction in sports that could be used to lead young men to a good end."

His life's calling slowly came into focus, and then one day it all clicked. During an intense moment on the football field, a fellow offensive lineman unleashed a stream of profanity. Turning to his right, the footballer saw Naismith and immediately stopped swearing. "I beg your pardon, Jim," he said. "I forgot you were there." It was another life-changing moment for Naismith. His pulpit would not be found in a church, but on the fields of play. "I never said a word about his profanity, and I could not understand why he should have apologized to me," Naismith recalled. "Later, thinking the matter over, the only reason that I could give for [his] action was that I played the game with all my might and yet held myself under control." For Naismith, the message was clear: there were other ways of doing good besides preaching. He understood the ministry, but also the common man. He could bring young men closer to God through athletics.

James Naismith wasn't the only person coming to this conclusion in the late 1800s. In fact, a name emerged to describe the philosophy he believed in: Muscular Christianity, a belief that vigorous physical activity strengthened a man's moral qualities, and in turn, created a stronger church and country. It was no coincidence that YMCAs were expanding their influence at the time.

Advocates of Muscular Christianity believed a nation of strong, fit, self-made men of the highest character would be a great nation indeed. It was during this period that the country's keen interest in physical education resulted in the creation of scholastic varsity athletic programs, country clubs, and the Amateur Athletic Union (AAU). Internationally, when Pierre de Coubertin of France revived the ancient Olympic Games in 1896, he called on a deep understanding of the Muscular Christian ideal.

The director of the YMCA in Montreal recommended Naismith investigate the School for Christian Workers in Springfield, Massachusetts, which was establishing a training program for future YMCA directors (the school would soon become known as the International YMCA Training School and then Springfield College).

Intrigued, Naismith traveled to Springfield and walked into a redbrick building at the corner of State and Sherman Streets. Here he met twenty-five-year-old Gulick—tall, red-haired, blue-eyed, full of vigor. He told Gulick he was interested in keeping men away from vice and sin, that his motto was "Do good and be pure." Gulick shared his interest in bringing together spirituality, science, and athletics, and his strong belief in the value of play and games.

Naismith found himself surrounded by like-minded, progressive thinkers and doers. While sports were still considered a diabolical pursuit by some, from Springfield emerged a school of thought, whether true or not, that many Americans take for granted today: that sports provide a positive outlet to channel aggression and competitiveness, that participants gain self-confidence and learn teamwork

*Japanese student G.S. Ishikawa created this sketch of the first basketball game ever played. Every single basketball game in history stems from this first action in Springfield, Massachusetts, on December 21, 1891.* (Springfield College Archives & Special Collections)

and sportsmanship, and that these lessons can be transferred to daily life. From this small school—sharing space in a building that also housed the Armory Hill YMCA—emerged such staples of American life as basketball, volleyball, body-building, and scouting. Walk into any YMCA in the world and you'll see a logo prominently featuring an inverted triangle. It was invented by Luther Gulick. And the Y's commitment to "body, mind, and spirit," represented by the three sides of the triangle? A slogan introduced by Gulick in Springfield.

It was with all this as surrounding context that Naismith blurted out that he could invent a new game. Within weeks, he stood on a ladder, nailing two peach baskets to the edge of an elevated running track that stood ten feet off the ground in the school's basement gymnasium.

Eighteen men, nine on the court for each team, played this new sport for the first time on December 21, 1891. Everything went great except for one thing. The game had no name. Someone suggested Naismithball. No way, said the inventor. Then Frank Mahan, one of the first students to play the game, came up with another idea.

What if they called it "basket ball"?

# CHAPTER FIVE

# Man on a Mission

I t's a long way from a basement gymnasium in western Massachusetts to the Olympic Games.

In the days before television, the Internet, cell phones, and texting, how did a sport invented by one man for one class of students at one small school become so quickly known, understood, and played by people all over the world? And, with better known sports such as baseball, football, lacrosse, and rugby *not* on the Olympic program, how did basketball make the cut just forty-five years after its invention?

The answer goes back to that first game. Remember, this was an *international* training school with many foreign students. Its purpose was to prepare these students to run YMCAs all over the world, many of which encountered the same challenge that flummoxed the instructors in Springfield: how to keep restless young men physically active during the long, dark days of winter.

So, while the game quickly became a community attraction in Springfield—within two weeks, as many as two hundred people packed the gym to watch, including female schoolteachers, who soon created their own team—it also found receptive audiences across the globe.

The catalyst was an article in Luther Gulick's magazine, *The Triangle*, which he mailed to YMCA directors worldwide. There on page 144 of the January 15, 1892, issue was an unassuming headline, "BASKET BALL," beneath a sketch depicting the first game, drawn by a witness, student G.S. Ishikawa of Tokyo, Japan.

The author of the article was James Naismith, and, in addition to sharing his original thirteen rules, here's how he described his invention.

"We present to our readers a new game of ball . . . Any number of men may play it, and each one gets plenty of exercise; at the same time, it calls for physical judgment, and co-ordination of every muscle, and gives all-around development. It can be played by teams from different Associations, and combines skill with courage and agility so that the better team wins . . . This game is interesting to spectators as well as to the players . . . It is intended that this game should be free from much of the reputed roughness of Rugby . . . There is neither science nor skill in taking a man unawares, and shoving him, or catching his arm and pulling him away, when he is about to catch the ball. A dog could do as much as that."

The new game caught on with lightning speed. As Springfield graduates took jobs at Ys around the world, they brought basketball with them. In less than two years, YMCA workers trained in Springfield introduced the game in a dozen countries. Duncan Patton brought basketball to India in 1894; Emil Thies to France in 1895; C. Herek to Persia in 1901; Chester Tobin to Turkey; Robert Galey to North China.

*The game of basketball spread quickly around the world in just the first few years after Naismith invented it. In the early days, players still shot the ball into literal baskets.*
(Springfield College Archives & Special Collections)

The game received another international boost during World War I, when YMCA personnel assigned to U.S. military camps in Europe set up athletic contests to keep soldiers occupied and out of trouble when they weren't engaged in battle. Basketball was one of the most popular pastimes, and the Americans shared the game with their European allies. At the end of the war, a kind of mini-Olympics in Paris known as the Inter-Allied Games brought together soldiers from eighteen nations. The U.S. defeated France and Italy to win the basketball tournament.

Even before the war, the game appeared in international settings. At the 1904 Olympics in St. Louis, basketball was introduced as an unofficial "demonstration sport," with American teams competing against one another in three divisions: high school, college, and professional. The best team in the pro tournament was a group of German-American immigrants from the East Side YMCA in Buffalo, New York. They called themselves the Buffalo Germans, and they were legendary in the early twentieth century, winning 111 straight games from 1908–1911.

Shortly after the Buffalo team's 1904 victory in St. Louis, a nineteen-year-old boy in Independence, Missouri, began taunting the "world champs," challenging them to come back to the Midwest to defend their title. The teenager convinced investors to rent the convention hall in Kansas City for a three-game series between his team, the Kansas City Athletic Club, and the squad from Buffalo. The young man and the investors would split any profit from ticket sales at the five-thousand-seat venue.

The Buffalo Germans accepted the challenge (and $600) and traveled to Kansas City. They won the first game and lost the second. Playing with two broken elbows, the five-foot-eleven teenage organizer led his Kansas City team to a 45–14 blowout win in game three. The referee in the third and deciding game was none other than James Naismith, by that point the physical education director at the University of Kansas. And the nineteen-year-old kid at the center of the spectacle? Later in life, he'd be better known by his nickname than his given name, and the basketball field house at his alma mater would be named in his honor. He remains one of the most influential figures in the history of basketball. Naismith, in fact, called him the "father of basketball coaching." And, most important for the purposes of this story, no single individual was more responsible for basketball's inclusion in the 1936 Olympic Games. His name was Forrest "Phog" Allen.

Where Naismith valued basketball primarily as a form of physical fitness, it was Allen, head coach at the University of Kansas for thirty-nine years, who envisioned what we now understand as the totality of the modern game: exercise for the participants, yes, but also high-level coaching, tournament action, massive spectator interest, a way to make money. Nothing embodies this vision of basketball better than the NCAA Tournament—March Madness—so it should come as no surprise that it was Allen, through the National Association of Basketball Coaches, which he founded, who created the tournament in 1939.

As he worked to elevate the sport of basketball to its highest potential, Allen took a keen interest in the Olympic Games. Beginning in 1928, he contacted officials in the U.S. and around the world (many of whom were graduates of Springfield College) to lobby for basketball's inclusion at the 1932 Games in

*Not only was Phog Allen a legendary college basketball coach, he was also a driving force behind the acceptance of basketball as an Olympic sport and the creation of the NCAA Tournament.* (University of Kansas Spencer Research Library)

Los Angeles, even if just as a demonstration sport, as had been done in St. Louis in 1904, Paris in 1924, and Amsterdam in 1928. By October of 1929, however, Allen had resigned himself to the fact that it wasn't going to happen. The LA committee chose American football instead. Even though hardly any other countries played football, organizers believed they could draw a big crowd at the LA Coliseum for an All-Star game between American college players, and the promise of lucrative ticket sales overshadowed any other considerations.

Undeterred, Allen attended the LA Olympics to meet with athletic officials from other countries and gain their support for basketball at future Olympics. Among his key meetings were lunch with German Olympic official Carl Diem and dinner with a Japanese basketball advocate, Sohaku Ri. With Tokyo slated to host the Olympics in 1940, Ri promised to lobby his German counterparts for '36, and all but assured Allen that basketball would be included in Japan if the Germans didn't bite.

*Carl Diem was the most influential sports figure in Germany for decades before, during, and after the Nazi regime. He admired the American approach to amateur sports and wrote a letter to Phog Allen to let him know basketball had been added to the '36 Games.* (U.S. Holocaust Memorial Museum, courtesy of Gerhard Vogel)

Allen worked other German contacts, too, including Fritz Sieweke, an exchange student Allen had counseled during a summer basketball camp at Springfield College. Sieweke was now back in Germany working for the Hitler Youth, a sinister organization that indoctrinated German boys in Nazi culture. Basketball wasn't a popular sport in Germany at the time, but Sieweke pressed the case. Allen also continued to lobby Diem, secretary general of the Berlin Organizing Committee and one of the most powerful sports officials in Germany. Diem had visited the U.S. often, had many American friends, and admired the U.S. approach to athletics so much that he founded an equivalent to the YMCA Training School known as the German College of Physical Education.

Ultimately, German Olympic officials decided not to include basketball as one of the demonstration sports in 1936, selecting glider flying and field handball instead. Much to Allen's delight, basketball was chosen as a full medal sport. An October 25, 1934, letter from Diem to Allen confirmed it—and gave the Kansas coach credit. "I have the pleasure of informing you," Diem wrote, "that the Organizing Committee at its meeting October 19, adopted the resolution that basketball be included in the program of the 1936 Olympic Games in Berlin . . . Thanking you again for your kind suggestion."

For Allen, years of dogged lobbying, networking, and fact-finding across multiple continents had paid off. Where his own countrymen had let him down by shunning basketball in Los Angeles, the Nazis lifted basketball onto the international stage. Writing confidentially to his ally Ri in Tokyo in August of 1935, Allen admitted the Nazi connection gave him reason for concern, if not for humanitarian reasons then for the potential damage to his favorite sport. "Yes, we are elated over the fact that basket ball is to become an Olympic sport," he said. "I am sincerely anxious that nothing shall happen in Berlin to cause the postponement of our games on account of the . . . Jewish difficulties that are taking place over there."

While Allen fretted over the possibility of Nazi atrocities interfering with the Olympic basketball tournament, millions of other Americans questioned the morality of holding the Olympics in Germany at all.

The United States of America, they argued, should take a stand for freedom.

It should boycott the Nazi Games.

# CHAPTER SIX

# The Boycott Question

A man is not defined by the documents on his desk, but consider the hateful, anti-Semitic material that Avery Brundage, president of the American Olympic Committee and the country's most powerful figure in amateur sports, kept at his Chicago office. There was a "pro-American" pamphlet that equated patriotism with hatred of Jewish people. There was another propaganda journal with the bizarre headline, "The Proof of a Jewish Conspiracy to Communize America and Rule the World." And there was a copy of a speech Brundage saved titled "Why We Should Oppose the Jew."

It was Brundage who pushed the hardest for American participation in the 1936 Olympics, leading a vigorous campaign against those who believed the U.S. should boycott the Olympics in protest of the brutal Nazi regime.

*Avery Brundage competed in the 1912 Olympics in the pentathlon and decathlon. By 1928, he became president of the American Olympic Committee. An anti-Semite, Brundage pushed hard for American participation in Berlin and cynically mocked U.S. opponents of Nazism. Even after supporting the Nazis, Brundage was rewarded with the presidency of the International Olympic Committee in 1952.*
(U.S. Holocaust Memorial Museum, courtesy of Gerhard Vogel)

Brundage, a former Olympic decathlete himself in the 1912 Games, claimed that the Olympics were purely a sporting event, that politics should be kept out, and that he and other Olympic leaders had no right to meddle in the internal affairs of the host country. Besides, he argued, the Games belonged to the International Olympic Committee (IOC), not the Nazis; Germany was merely the host. There were problems with all aspects of Brundage's reasoning. First, as we shall see, he didn't abide by the "don't meddle with another country" rule himself. Second, the Nazis were intimately involved in planning the Berlin Olympics. These were every bit their Games. Finally, the idea that sports and politics are separate entities has repeatedly been proven false. Political considerations related to race, gender, religion, nationality, social status, and sexuality have determined who can play, what they can play, where they can play, and how much they can earn for centuries.

To be fair, there was some merit to Brundage's steadfast insistence on moving forward with the Olympics regardless of the politics of the moment. As an athletic administrator, his primary interest was in ensuring the longevity and success of the Games, not solving the world's humanitarian problems. Still, given his personal biases, it was clear there was a strong measure of anti-Semitism underlying Brundage's position, not to mention hypocrisy: no one had ever exploited the Olympics for political purposes more than Adolf Hitler and the Nazis. Their aim was to use the Games to create enthusiasm for the regime at home and to positively influence international opinion.

There was also a dose of pure self-interest behind the wealthy Brundage's support of the Nazi Games. Just as many public officials throughout history have considered their own personal fortunes when making decisions that affect large groups of people, Brundage looked out for himself even as he publicly spoke of lofty Olympic and American ideals. His construction company was in line to build a new German embassy in Washington, DC. Pulling the U.S. Olympic team out of the Berlin Games wouldn't be good for business.

Brundage's closest pro-participation ally was an International Olympic Committee member and former U.S. ambassador to Turkey named Charles Sherrill, a Yale-educated Hitler admirer who saw it as his mission to convince the dictator to include at least one token Jewish person on the German Olympic team to make it harder for opponents to claim discrimination. As a personal guest of Hitler, Sherrill attended an infamous Nazi Party rally in Nuremberg, Germany, in 1935 where Hitler stripped Jewish people of their German citizenship. The American came away not with condemnation for this heinous act, but with admiration for the entire spectacle. Shamefully, Sherrill even threatened Jewish people in the U.S., suggesting that their opposition to participation in the '36 Games would make them the targets of anti-Semitic retaliation from their fellow Americans.

Brundage had visited Germany in 1934, supposedly to see for himself if there was discrimination against Jewish athletes. But his trip was a farce. His host was an old Nazi pal, Karl Ritter von Halt, who not only translated for Brundage but also handpicked all the people he interviewed. When Brundage spoke to a group of Jewish people at Berlin's Kaiserhof Hotel, standing behind him was an intimidating Nazi SS officer in a black uniform. Brundage was so concerned his visit might worry his Nazi hosts that he soothed their anti-Semitic feelings by reminding them his men's club in Chicago did not admit Jewish people, either. He had no interest in "fact-finding" on this trip and later admitted so. "Frankly, I don't think we have any business meddling in this question," he told the *New York Times* in 1935. If the saying is true, that all that is required for evil to prosper is for good people to do nothing, then here was a clear example of a powerful and widely respected American choosing not to take a stand for human rights. "We are a sports group, organized and pledged to promote clean competition and sportsmanship." Brundage shrugged. "When we let politics, racial questions, religious or social disputes creep into our actions, we're in for trouble and plenty of it."

On the other side of the debate were prominent figures such as George Messersmith, head of the U.S. Consulate in Germany; Jeremiah Mahoney, president of the Amateur Athletic Union; and Rabbi Stephen Wise of New York, each of whom strongly objected to U.S. participation in the Nazi Olympics.

A career diplomat from Pennsylvania, Messersmith identified the looming Nazi threat to world peace earlier than most in the U.S. government, writing to the State Department in 1933 that many Nazi leaders were "psychopaths" bent on war. Incensed that Brundage and Sherrill were uninterested in acknowledging the true conditions in Germany and were willingly misleading the American public, he sent cables to U.S. Secretary of State Cordell Hull in hopes that accurate information would educate the general public and the decision makers at the American Olympic Committee and Amateur Athletic Union who would ultimately decide whether the U.S. would boycott or participate. He reported that Jewish people had been kicked out of German sports organizations and anticipated that the Nazis would allow a token Jewish person or two to participate in Olympic training programs, warning that "this will be merely a screen for the real discrimination which is taking place."

But Messersmith's reports were ignored, even when he suggested that a U.S. boycott would do considerable damage to Nazi prestige at home and abroad. Secretary of State Hull responded to just one of Messersmith's numerous reports, and that was only to say that the administration was going to stay out of the Olympic matter.

As a respected New York judge and president of the AAU, the country's most influential amateur sports organization, Mahoney held considerable sway in American athletic circles. Mahoney was a defender of civil rights and found it unconscionable that America would send its athletes to Hitler's Germany. He said it was hypocritical for Brundage to claim supporters of the boycott were introducing politics into sports.

*A New York City pedestrian stops to read posters advertising a rally supporting the proposed Olympic boycott. Many Americans believed it was wrong to participate in an Olympics hosted by Adolf Hitler's fascist regime.* (U.S. Holocaust Memorial Museum, courtesy of National Archives)

"I wish to say to Mr. Brundage—and he knows it as well as I do—that it is we who are trying to keep politics out of sport," he said. "And the worst and rottenest kind of politics, the politics of Nazism, the politics of organized prejudice, the politics of crazy radicalism, which has robbed the German people of freedom . . . I am ashamed to think that any American might possibly go to Berlin and take part in the Olympics."

In New York City, Rabbi Wise of the city's Free Synagogue became one of the leading Jewish voices against American participation in the Games. Standing before his congregation of two thousand at Carnegie Hall on November 3, 1935, he delivered a passionate sermon titled "The Berlin Olympics: The Truth and Some Lies." Wise framed opposition to the Nazis not as a Jewish question but as an American one. All the freedoms Americans believe, stand for, and have fought and died for, he said, were challenged by the Nazis. "If America goes to the Olympic Games," he said, "the world will remember it to our dishonor and our shame. If we valiantly withdraw from the Olympics, history will say under valiant leadership America did what America's best and highest can always be counted on to do. Namely to seek the right, to pursue the way of justice."

At its core, the boycott debate centered around a question of American values. Both sides would claim they were defending American principles.

Boycott supporters pointed to America as a land of determined immigrants founded on the notion of religious freedom. They viewed the persecution of Jewish Germans as a threat to human rights everywhere. Their America could not in good conscience compete in the spirit of fair play and sportsmanship in a

*Well before the U.S. participated in the 1936 Olympics or entered World War II in 1941, many Americans understood the Nazi regime was a dangerous threat to human rights around the world. In 1933, more than 100,000 people marched through the streets of New York protesting Nazi policies.* (U.S. Holocaust Memorial Museum, courtesy of American Jewish Congress)

despotic dictatorship that stood starkly against everything that made the United States exceptional.

On the pro-participation side were those who said the U.S. had no business "meddling" in the political affairs of another nation when it came to a sporting event. And there were also those who simply enjoyed the idea of the Olympic Games and didn't want American athletes denied the opportunity to compete. But there was also a strong strain of ugliness to the arguments that portrayed boycott supporters as something other than "real Americans," a mind-set rooted in homegrown anti-Semitism. The Brundage brand of patriots took pride in their white, northern European, Protestant Christian heritage, adopting an isolationist view of the world that assumed the superiority of their country and their positions in life. Their America would not be prevented from demonstrating its prowess at the world's greatest athletic spectacle over the concerns of a vocal minority—Jewish people in America and Europe and their supporters.

Brundage received numerous letters of support from citizens who admired his position (at least one of which was signed *Heil Hitler/Heil Brundage*), and those letters revealed a lot about the mind-set of prejudiced Americans who had little interest in the evils of anti-Semitism or Nazism prior to World War II.

"Every fair minded American will stand behind you and your associates in resisting the pressure of an obnoxious, articulate minority to break faith with American youth who wish to participate in the Games," wrote Charles Estabrook of Chicago, who congratulated Brundage for his "sturdy Americanism." "It is a good man that attends to his own business, but the Jews have a weakness for mixing up in other people's business, the probable seat of all of their troubles."

Maude DeLand wrote to Brundage from Kansas City. "What has happened to the American people," she wrote, "that they do not have the courage to tell the Jews to keep their international troubles to themselves if they want to be considered good American citizens? I suppose they intend to dominate us as they did Germany until Hitler concluded that the Germans ought to have something to say in their own country."

Edward Smythe of the Federation of Independent Republicans copied

Brundage on a letter he wrote to boycott supporter Mahoney in which he called Mahoney a "tool" of the Jewish people. "The Jewish question in Germany is for the Germans to handle, not for us to butt into," he wrote. "If the Jew had behaved themselves there they would still be enjoying the freedom of Germany. You talk of TOLERANCE. Tolerance HELL, and to HELL with tolerance. The American people have been far too tolerant, and so they have been imposed upon."

For anyone who might say, *Well, Brundage couldn't control what people wrote to him and maybe he didn't believe all the anti-Semitic things people were writing in their letters*, consider Brundage's reply to Mrs. DeLand. "Thank you for your recent letter and the friendly sentiments contained therein," he wrote. "You have not exaggerated the situation and it is unfortunate that more Americans do not know what is going on in their own country." And to Smythe, he extended his thanks for blasting Mahoney "straight from the shoulder."

Public opinion on the matter was divided. A Gallup poll in March 1935 indicated 43 percent of Americans favored a boycott, a hefty percentage given this was the first time a U.S. boycott of an Olympics had ever been proposed. Many influential national newspaper columnists took pro-boycott positions. In the *Washington Post*, Shirley Povich wrote that "the only excuse for staging a 1936 Olympiad in Germany would be to equip Hitler with two 56-pound weights and let him set a new broad jump record that would land him at the bottom of the Rhine." In the Waterbury, Connecticut, *Evening Democrat*, columnist John Cluney wrote that Hitler's "cruel and merciless" anti-Semitism was an affront to American values. "It is a cardinal principle of true and loyal Americanism that all people should be permitted to worship God as they see fit," he wrote, "and that no particular race, creed or color shall ever be a necessary qualification for public honors or for the right to represent America, athletically or otherwise."

While President Roosevelt remained silent on the matter, maintaining the traditional American separation between the government and the Olympic movement, Pennsylvania governor George Earle said participation in the Nazi Games would send the wrong message to young people, that Hitler's regime stood in opposition to every ideal Americans hold dear. "If you want your children to be taught that might is right," he said, "that woman is a lower animal than man, that free press, free speech and religious freedom are false ideals, that peace is weakness, that liberty as we have learned to love it in America is a myth—if you want these doctrines inculcated in the youth of America, then send your boys and girls to Germany."

# CHAPTER SEVEN

# Meddling in the Olympics

The possibility of an American withdrawal from the Games was of great concern to Olympic organizers and Nazi leaders in Berlin. Without talented American athletes, the sporting events would be severely compromised; without American visitors and media coverage, the propaganda value of the Games squandered.

With a shared interest in ensuring American participation, Brundage and his German counterparts worked closely to influence the outcome of the boycott debate in the States. In so doing, it was a betrayal of Brundage's stated values, an example of Olympic officials involving themselves in the internal affairs of a participating nation. Brundage and the Germans secretly worked together to shape American public opinion.

In a letter to Nazi sports leader Hans von Tschammer und Osten, Brundage stressed "the absolute necessity of your full cooperation in carrying on favorable Olympic propaganda in the United States." He also wrote to Carl Diem, asking him to mail German newspaper articles featuring Jewish athletes training for the Olympics to "balance out" news of Nazi thuggery. "A few days ago," Brundage wrote, "there was a story in the newspapers that a Polish Jew participating in a [soccer] game against Germans had been killed by Nazis. You can imagine the result of such stories, particularly when at least 90 [percent] of the people in the United States, as I informed you when I last saw you, are anti-Nazi."

A member of the German American Olympic Committee wrote directly to Nazi propaganda minister Joseph Goebbels asking for assistance. "It is necessary for the German Olympic Propaganda Committee to help me in creating favorable public opinion in this country to offset the large volume of adverse publicity."

*Nazi propaganda minister Joseph Goebbels, here with his wife, Magda, assumed complete control over all forms of media in Germany, including using the relatively new mediums of radio and film to shape public opinion. There was no free press—only government propaganda.* (U.S. Holocaust Memorial Museum, courtesy Wendie Theus)

On another occasion, Brundage's publicist, Clarence Bush, wrote to Carl Diem requesting a favor. Every time Brundage spoke in favor of U.S. participation, Nazi newspapers applauded, giving Brundage's American critics reason to complain about his Nazi allegiances. Tell the Nazi papers to just be quiet about it, Bush urged Diem.

The Nazis played their usual games with language and the truth when it came to the question of whether they would allow Jewish athletes to try out for the German Olympic team. *One must be a member of an official German sports organization to be considered for the Olympics.* But Jewish people were barred from the clubs. *Jewish people aren't banned, they're just not good enough to make the team.* In this lie, the Nazis were joined by Frederick Rubien, secretary of the American Olympic Committee. "Germans are not discriminating against Jews in their Olympic trials," he falsely claimed. "The Jews are eliminated because they are not good enough as athletes. Why, there are not a dozen Jews in the world of Olympic calibre—and not one in our winter sports that I know of." Rubien overlooked the fact that in the 1932 Winter Olympics in Lake Placid, New York, American Irving Jaffee, the son of Jewish immigrants from Russia, won two gold medals in speed skating, joining teammate Jack Shea as the first Americans ever to win two golds at a Winter Olympics. A total of twenty-three Jewish people had medaled at the 1932 Winter and Summer Games.

In the end, to appease international critics, German fencer Helene Mayer, whose father was Jewish and mother Lutheran, was invited to compete for Germany, a suggestion proposed by American Charles Sherrill. The blond-haired, blue-eyed Mayer, who had been living in Los Angeles for a year, just a few blocks away from U.S. basketball player Sam Balter, accepted the invitation. Still, Goebbels's propaganda ministry demanded German newspapers not mention Mayer's "non-Aryan descent."

Then there was the case of Gretel Bergmann, one of the most accomplished athletes in Germany, a record-setting Jewish high jumper. German authorities gave Bergmann the impression she'd have a chance to represent her country in the Olympics, summoning her home in 1934 from England, where she had lived for a year to evade Nazi persecution. Having just won the British championships, Bergmann performed extremely well over the course of the next two years in Germany, winning meets in Ulm and Munich as the Olympics drew near. But she wasn't allowed to compete at the German national qualifying meet just prior to the Games. On July 16, one day after the American Olympians began their sea voyage to Germany, and after it was too late for the U.S. to protest, the Germans kicked Bergmann off their Olympic team. They mailed her a letter to break the news, adding further insult by inviting her to come watch the track events with standing-room-only tickets. The letter was signed *Heil Hitler*.

It was obvious to Bergmann the Nazis had used her for propaganda purposes all along, giving the world the impression they were allowing a Jewish person the opportunity to make their team even though there was never any intent to let her compete in Berlin. Bergmann read the letter while sitting on the front steps of her house. She went inside, dropped the page on the dining room table, and went upstairs to lie down on her bed, fuming mad. "It was hard for me to accept that

*Gretel Bergmann was one of the greatest athletes in Germany in the early 1930s. But because she was Jewish, the Nazis prevented her from competing in the 1936 Olympics. She emigrated to the United States in 1937 and died in New York in 2017 at the age of 103.* (U.S. Holocaust Memorial Museum, courtesy of Mel Hecker)

within less than 60 seconds, the time it took to read the fateful words, my aspirations had been shattered," she recalled. "Damn it, I was one of the four best high jumpers in the world and only through an accident of birth, having been born Jewish, I was being cast aside like an old shoe."

In the end, Brundage was the victor. The AAU voted in support of participation. Americans competed in the '36 Games; there was no boycott. American athletes overwhelmingly supported the decision; one doesn't get many chances to compete on the world's largest stage. There were no commercial endorsements at stake, no big paydays. Many athletes, including the basketball players, were told they'd lose their jobs if they took time off to compete in the Olympics. They competed because they loved their sport and wanted to test themselves against the best in the world. Should they have been denied that opportunity?

And for Americans of color, there was another wrinkle to the boycott argument.

Where was this passion for the civil rights of minorities when it came to inequalities in their own country? Forbidden relationships, social ostracism, economic strangulation, political powerlessness, a rigged legal system, racially motivated violence, ugly stereotypes, segregated athletics, second-class citizenship—it all sounded awfully familiar.

# CHAPTER EIGHT

# Mirror, Mirror

It was a February afternoon, five years before the 1936 Olympics and thousands of miles away. Men and women sat on park benches and discussed politics and the weather. Their children played nearby. The Great Depression made life difficult for these people, but they persevered, working hard, saving money, dreaming of a better future.

Because of their ancestry, the families at the park existed on the fringes of society, looked down on by the majority, made to feel inferior, told they were taking jobs from "more deserving" citizens. Newspaper advertisements urged them to leave the country.

It was an ordinary afternoon—then suddenly it wasn't. Women screamed. Children watched helplessly as men carrying guns and clubs accosted their mothers and fathers. People got up and ran, but there was nowhere to go, the entire park blocked by undercover government agents. More than four hundred people were captured, loaded into vans, and eventually packed into trains and deported, families torn apart in an instant.

This wasn't Berlin, this wasn't Nazi Germany, and these people weren't Jewish.

The park was called La Placita, and it was in Los Angeles, California.

The men and women were Mexican Americans. The surprise raid on February 26, 1931, was carried out by the U.S. government, the first in a series of shameful attacks that would ultimately drive more than one million people out of the country, more than half of whom had been born in the U.S., including one-third of the Mexican population of Los Angeles.

When Olympic athletes from Mexico arrived in Los Angeles a year later for the 1932 Games, they were turned away from the same restaurants where other teams dined, as were the Japanese. Black and Latino citizens were banned from the city's public parks and swimming pools.

And California was considered a land of freedom, a sunny paradise where dreams came true.

It was no Florida, where in 1934, fourteen carloads of white men attacked Robert Johnson, a black man who had been accused of stealing chickens, mercilessly beating and kicking him before dragging him into a field and riddling his lifeless body with gunfire.

It was no Georgia, where just three months before the 1936 Olympics, a mob of white men accosted a black man named Lint Shaw. The mob paraded Shaw in

*Throughout the United States in the early 1930s, people of Mexican descent—the majority of them U.S. citizens— were routinely rounded up in public places and deported to Mexico. Here, friends and relatives wave goodbye to a train carrying 1,500 people being expelled from Los Angeles to Mexico in August 1931.* (Getty Images)

front of his house, where his wife and children huddled in fear, and then hung him from a nearby tree before piercing his body with bullets.

It wasn't even Lawrence, Kansas, home of the state's flagship university. The University of Kansas, where Phog Allen and James Naismith worked, barred black students from participating in everything from sports to the band to the debate team. Black students couldn't live on campus or go to school dances and were confined to a segregated balcony at concerts. No segregated fraternity or sorority would accept them.

To be black or Latino or Asian or Native American in the United States of America in the 1930s meant living in a land that boasted of freedom, liberty, and equality but offered domestic terrorism instead. Black people were murdered by white mobs with impunity in the South—an average of one lynching every two weeks during the first three years of the presidency of Franklin D. Roosevelt—and members of Congress bragged they would do nothing to curb the lawlessness. American bigotry, whether focused on skin color or religion, was all connected.

This cloud of white supremacy hovered over the Olympic participation debate, hampering the boycott effort on two flanks. There were the racists with little interest in opposing anti-Semitism on one hand and the social progressives whose attention was diverted stateside on the other. Syndicated newspaper columnist Westbrook Pegler recognized the element of hypocrisy inherent in condemnations of German anti-Semitism, writing that America's own racism "causes the pointing finger of scorn to waver somewhat." Black political leaders and newspapers were of mixed minds. Some claimed that bigotry and discrimination needed to be confronted wherever they existed, and that black people should take a stand for human rights by boycotting the Nazi Games. Others claimed the U.S. should solve its own problems before demanding change abroad. Besides, the best way to counter racism, they believed, was through undeniable achievements. Gold medals in Berlin would refute claims of white supremacy.

Regardless of the ways people in the U.S. viewed the situation in Germany, the uncomfortable truth is that the Nazis were looking right back, nodding with approval at the ugliest aspects of American life. When crafting the 1935 Nuremberg Laws, which denied Jewish people their citizenship, the Nazis looked to U.S. law and culture for precedent and inspiration. As Yale law professor James Q. Whitman writes in his book *Hitler's American Model*, "the American impact on the rest of the world is not limited to what makes Americans proudest about their country. It has also included aspects of the American past that we might prefer to forget."

This included Hitler's admiration for the genocidal killing and banishment to reservations of "inferior" Native Americans, as well as race-based American immigration laws that gave preferential treatment to white people over darker-skinned people. In crafting laws that pertained to immigration, citizenship, sex, and marriage, Nazi lawyers went looking around the world for precedent and found it, Whitman writes, in the United States. On "race-mixing," the U.S. stood nearly alone in the world in its bigotry, with laws criminalizing interracial marriage or sexual relations on the books in thirty states. (These laws, shamefully, were rarely if ever enforced when white men raped black women.)

*Racism was a part of everyday life in America, and the Nazis knew it. They studied American race law when crafting their own racist policies. Here, hooded members of the Ku Klux Klan parade through the streets of McPherson, Kansas, in 1929.* (McPherson Public Library)

*Racial terrorism wasn't just a fact of life in Nazi Germany. In the United States, the NAACP office in New York brought attention to the vigilante murder of African Americans by white people, hanging a flag from its window every time there was a lynching in the U.S. (Shutterstock.com)*

While the Nazis weren't overly interested in racial segregation as it was practiced in many parts of the U.S., there were aspects of Southern racism that were nearly indistinguishable from Nazi brutality. Whitman quotes American historians who wrote that in the early 1930s Nazi Germany and the American South were a "mirror image" of each other, "two unapologetically racist regimes, unmatched in their pitilessness. In the early 1930s, the Jewish people of Germany were hounded, beaten, and sometimes murdered by mobs and by the state alike. In the same years the black people of the American South were hounded, beaten, and sometimes murdered as well."

All this is not to say Nazis admired everything about the United States. Far from it. Not free and open elections, not a free press, not freedom of religion, not freedom of speech, not an independent judicial system, nor even capitalism. The same America that profited from slavery and gave rise to the KKK also produced Frederick Douglass and Susan B. Anthony and a Constitution unlike anything in history. The same government that massacred Native Americans also declared that all men are created equal.

Recognizing the contradictions in America between everyday racism and ideals of freedom and equality, the Nazis held out hope in the early 1930s that the U.S. would ultimately join them in a brotherhood of white supremacy. But they profoundly miscalculated and, less than a decade after the Olympics, the Americans and their allies would destroy them in World War II.

And while the Nazis fiercely resisted allowing Jewish athletes to compete for Germany in '36, there were eighteen black people on the U.S. team, several of whom would distinguish themselves in Berlin, none more so than the great sprinter Jesse Owens of Ohio State University.

In all, African American athletes would win fourteen medals in Berlin. At an Olympics designed to showcase a white supremacist regime, black Americans were far and away the stars.

But that wasn't the only irony in Berlin. So let's now return to basketball, and consider the backstory of the Universal Pictures basketball team.

# CHAPTER NINE

# Hollywood Stars

This might sound odd, but to understand the origins and significance of the Universals, the Hollywood basketball team that made up half of the 1936 U.S. Olympic roster, it helps to know what happened at a Berlin movie theater on December 5, 1930, three years before the Nazis took control of Germany and six years before the Olympics.

Moviegoers at Berlin's Mozart Hall had just settled into their seats. The theater was full. *All Quiet on the Western Front*, an American film about the horror and senseless carnage of World War I, had received rave reviews in the U.S..

The theater went dark, the chattering died down, the movie was about to begin.

But then commotion: white mice squealed down the aisles, shrieking women jumped up on their seats, men shouted, "*Judenfilm! Judenfilm!* [Jewish film]," stink

Universal's 1930 movie All Quiet on the Western Front *portrayed the horrors of war, and was a hit in the* United States. *When it premiered in Germany, Joseph Goebbels and Nazi thugs—who opposed the antiwar message—disrupted the showing at Berlin's Mozart Hall with mice, powder, and shouts. (Universal Studios Licensing LLC)*

bombs filled the air. Then more mice and shouting, and violence, too, a few men roughed up, and some laughter and confusion, and the show was canceled.

Joseph Goebbels and his Nazi henchmen slipped out of the theater and made their way to a nearby café, where they laughed about the ruckus they'd created, having blended in with regular theatergoers. The Nazis were still three years away from power, but here was unmistakable evidence they could get away with whatever they wanted out in the streets.

They hated the movie and its antiwar message. And they hated the man who'd made it, Carl Laemmle. Though he had lived in the United States for nearly fifty years, Laemmle had been born in Laupheim, Germany. He was the founder of Universal Pictures in Hollywood. And he was Jewish.

Laemmle loved the Germany he had grown up in, returned often to visit, and had even built a thriving Universal office in Berlin. He was stunned by the reaction to the film in his homeland. But that night of bullying had been just the beginning. When the Nazis gained power in 1933, they censored and controlled all aspects of media and popular culture, including moviemaking, requiring scripts to honor the regime and forcing Jewish people out of jobs in the industry. By 1934, Laemmle shut down Universal's operations in Berlin.

Which made it ironic, as the United States basketball team sailed to Germany to compete in a tournament the Nazis had authorized, that half of the American players came from a team sponsored by Carl Laemmle and Universal Pictures.

Laemmle had sailed across the Atlantic in the opposite direction in 1884, from Europe to America, at age seventeen. With just $50 in his pocket, he was drawn, like so many other immigrants past and present, by the promise of America, the idea that through hard work he could build a better life.

For two decades, he toiled away at mundane jobs in the Midwest: store clerk, farmhand, bookkeeper. Then, on a visit to Chicago in 1906, he was intrigued by a long line of customers waiting to see a motion picture at one of the Windy City's "nickelodeons," theaters that showed movies for five cents. The thirty-nine-year-old Laemmle decided to strike out on his own, opening a 190-seat theater on Milwaukee Avenue in Chicago. But there was more money to be made in actually creating and distributing the films he showed and, inspired by a delivery wagon bearing the name "Universal Pipe Fitters," he named his creation Universal Film Manufacturing Company. By 1915, he had created Universal City in California, the world's first large-scale studio, complete with its own post office, fire department, and police station. More than three hundred people lived there, including Native Americans who appeared in the studio's many Westerns, several members of Laemmle's family, and other German immigrants. An Old West town one day, a French village the next, Laemmle dubbed Universal City the "strangest place on earth." Bus lines brought thousands of tourists to the studio, where they crammed into bleachers and watched the movies being made. Hollywood was born.

Laemmle was generous with his wealth, providing jobs to any family member who needed one. He built an egg ranch on the movie lot so relatives without useful skills could have a job, too. In 1932, when his adopted hometown of Los Angeles hosted the summer Olympics, Germany (not yet under Nazi rule) was mired in the Depression and didn't have the money to send a team to America. Laemmle took the lead raising funds. The German Olympic team came to LA largely due to his efforts.

*Carl Laemmle emigrated from Germany to the United States in 1884. In 1906 he opened his first movie theater in Chicago, and less than a decade later, he opened a studio in Los Angeles. He remains one of the most important figures in the creation of the American movie industry, and today you can find his star on the Hollywood Walk of Fame.* (Universal Studios Licensing LLC)

He had been bitten by the sports bug. When his chief makeup artist at the studio, Jack Pierce, came to him looking to sponsor a basketball team, he jumped at the chance. While the studio turned out popular, low-budget hits and horror films such as *The Hunchback of Notre Dame*, *The Phantom of the Opera*, and *Frankenstein*, Pierce's basketball team challenged opponents on the West Coast as a member of the Amateur Athletic Union, playing its home games before crowds of up to ten thousand in the Grand Olympic Auditorium. Today we recognize AAU basketball as a circuit where top high school stars showcase their skills, but back in the 1930s, before the advent of professional basketball, the AAU was entirely different. These teams were essentially semipro All-Star teams made up of former collegiate players who maintained their amateur status by technically being paid not to play basketball, but for "day jobs" with the team sponsor. In the case of Universal, that meant Pierce lined many of his guys up with odd jobs around the studio. They were the tallest group of stagehands in history.

Pierce was an unlikely basketball organizer, a former actor who became a makeup artist in the 1920s during the height of the silent film era. He was a stubby little guy with a narrow mustache, and though he never played basketball, he loved the sport and recognized the marketing opportunity that came with sponsoring a team. (His players' warm-up suits featured a patch of a popular Universal cartoon character known as Oswald the Rabbit, the creation of animator Walt Disney a year before he came up with a mouse named Mickey.)

Scouring the West Coast for talented ballplayers, Pierce found guys like Art Mollner who worked at the post office, whose parents had made a living singing and dancing in New York before moving to California for the better climate. Art picked up basketball in high school and starred at LA Junior College, where as a defensive specialist he always lined up opposite the other team's top scorer.

*Jack Pierce was the head makeup artist at Universal and the manager of the studio's champion basketball team. Here he puts the finishing touches on the* The Wolf Man *character for actor Lon Chaney. (*Universal Studios Licensing LLC)

In addition to Mollner, Pierce rounded out the team with a group of unlikely characters. Here are some of their stories.

Ever notice how some people make the most ridiculous decisions and everything still works out perfectly for them? That was the case for Duane Swanson. As a member of the freshman basketball team at the University of Iowa, Swanson and a friend hatched the idea that they would drop out of school and transfer to the University of Southern California. They went so far as to ship their belongings to Los Angeles and hitchhike across the country to their new home. Problem was, they didn't tell the coach at USC they were coming, and he didn't want them. No problem. Swanson hooked up with an AAU team sponsored by one of the most famous comedians in the movies, married a Hollywood actress, and, because Pierce convinced him to play for Universal in 1936, found himself on the United States Olympic team.

The fact that Frank Lubin was headed to Germany required another improbable chain of events. Lubin grew up in East Los Angeles as the son of Lithuanian immigrants. When a growth spurt shot him up to six foot five in high school, a classmate coaxed him onto the basketball team, but he wasn't interested in the game. Even at UCLA, he rarely made it off the bench. His style was so awkward he was known, unceremoniously, as the Lumberin' Lithuanian. By 1933, Lubin was struggling his way through law school in the Bay Area. His father's tailoring business had gone under. With poor grades, no money, and his family counting on him, Lubin felt hopeless. He moved home to LA to look for a job. A giant, out-of-work former college basketball player was just the man Jack Pierce was looking for. Pierce found him a job as an electrician at Universal and a spot on his basketball team. The good fortune continued. First, one of Universal's star players hired a personal coach for Lubin, helping him dramatically improve his offensive skills. He learned how to go left, how to go right, how to back his defender under the basket and score. Next, Lubin gained a bit of fame and a nickname. With Universal promoting its film *Bride of Frankenstein*, Pierce came up with an idea to generate interest. Before each game, he'd cover the six-foot-seven Lubin in green makeup and dress him in a frayed coat with metal bolts around his neck. Standing over seven feet tall in six-inch-high boots, "Frankenstein" Lubin would come out and

*Frank Lubin wasn't a great basketball player when he arrived at UCLA, but he improved his skills there and kept playing ball even after he graduated. Jack Pierce invited him to join the Universal team, and by 1936 he was considered one of the best players in the world. To this day, he is considered the father of basketball in his ancestral homeland of Lithuania.* (Los Angeles Public Library)

entertain the crowd before tip-off, then head back to the locker room and hurriedly change into his basketball uniform.

Then there was the coach. Any legendary basketball team must have an iconic coach, an unquestioned leader, an unshakable disciplinarian who inspires confidence by his very existence. Right?

Not so much with this bunch.

The Universals had only met Jimmy Needles, a former college coach, three months before the Olympics. They'd played the entire regular season without any coach at all and had done just fine. Needles didn't join the team until the post-season, and that was only because Braven Dyer, sports editor at the *Los Angeles Times*, felt sorry for him. Needles was out of work, depressed, looking for a way to stay involved in the game. Dyer recommended Needles to Pierce, who was busy with work at the studio and wouldn't be able to accompany the team to the Olympic tryouts in New York or the Games in Germany should they advance. Pierce said sure, we can't pay him, but he's welcome to come along.

When Needles first appeared on the Universals bench, his players didn't much care for him or think they needed him. But now here he was, a man whose name would go down in history, the head coach of the first U.S. Olympic basketball team.

As a kid, Sammy Balter was always involved in some sort of outdoor activity—playing baseball, basketball, and football with friends in the neighborhood, occasionally punching his buddies in the nose. He became sports editor of his middle school newspaper and was such a good high school basketball player that in one game against a rival, he scored all seventeen points in his team's 17–6 victory. Every Saturday, Sam worked from seven a.m. to ten p.m. at Los Angeles's Grand Central Market. He hated the pungent smell of the deli so much he told his boss if he had to do this the rest of his life, he'd kill himself. At age fifteen, he graduated from high school and was drafted by Major League Baseball's Chicago White Sox. They offered him $50 a month to play minor-league ball. Balter said no thanks and enrolled at UCLA, where he acted in plays and wrote for the student newspaper, played intramural tennis and Ping-Pong, lettered in basketball for three years, and played baseball as a senior. One of his English teachers tried to keep him humble despite all this success. "Heroes!" The professor smirked. "They're like Christmas trees. First, they're decorated, and then they're tossed aside—sometimes only a day later."

*Sam Balter's parents escaped anti-Semitism in Belarus and settled in California to pursue the American Dream. Balter loved playing sports as a kid, and he eventually created a popular national sports radio show that was a precursor to ESPN and SportsCenter. (Carrie Kahn)*

Balter wasn't the best student—mostly Cs—but he graduated in 1929 and began teaching high school English and history. In 1935, when he was fired for making sarcastic remarks a parent found distasteful, he had a lot more time for basketball. He landed a government job with the National Youth Administration, hooked up with the Universal team, and began working odd jobs around the studio. Now Balter was a member of the U.S. Olympic basketball team.

And one more thing.

Sammy Balter, on his way to Nazi Germany, was Jewish.

# CHAPTER TEN

# Unrefined

Gene Johnson didn't care if you liked the way his Globe Refiners played ball. His team from McPherson, Kansas, which made up the other half of the 1936 Olympic basketball team, was different. Instead of walking the ball up the court, they ran as if their pants were on fire. They didn't sit back and wait on defense either but chased the ball all over the floor. His players were tall, fast, and aggressive, and looked good in their shiny new red, white, and blue uniforms. It takes a lot to be noticed when you play your ball games amid the wheat and oil fields of central Kansas. And Gene Johnson, about as subdued as a peacock, yearned to be noticed.

So when the coach of the rival Hutchinson Renos criticized Johnson by saying his Globe Refiners didn't play real basketball, Gene had an answer.

"Maybe not, but the kids love to play it, the crowds love to watch it and we always win so it's a darn good substitute."

The Refiners were the biggest thing to happen in McPherson since the discovery of oil in 1929, so it made sense the local oil refinery sponsored the team. Coach Johnson convinced executives at Globe Oil that sponsoring a basketball team would be a great way to promote their gasoline, with the boys in Globe uniforms playing their head-turning brand of ball in front of potential customers in Kansas City, Wichita, and Denver. *Keep Rollin' with Globe*, the advertisements boasted. The players earned $90 a month working at the refinery, though during basketball season hoops was pretty much their full-time job.

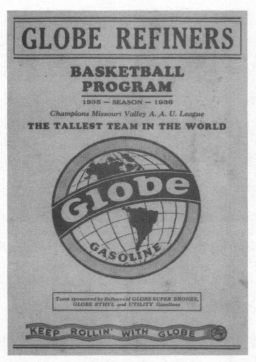

*A game program for the Globe Refiners boasted that they were the "Tallest Team in the World." With giant centers such as Joe Fortenberry and Willard Schmidt, it may have been an accurate claim.* (McPherson Museum)

Johnson's boys were heroes in McPherson, a town of around seven thousand along the old Santa Fe Trail, fifty-seven miles north of Wichita. In years past, McPhersonites had looked forward to spelling bees at the opera house, movies at the Ritz Theater, and roller-skating down by the Peterson dairy. But ever since Johnson arrived in 1934, Refiners games were the hottest thing in town. Tickets in Convention Hall were so hard to get that some people came to the gym just to watch the team practice. During ball games, more than 1,200 fans filled the gym, far exceeding the gym's legal seating capacity.

*Here's the Globe Oil Refinery in McPherson, Kansas. Members of the Refiners basketball team were paid for jobs at the refinery and not for playing basketball, thus technically preserving their amateur status, a necessary requirement to compete in the Olympics at the time.* (McPherson Public Library)

While tens of millions of people suffered from unemployment, low wages, poverty, and hunger during the Great Depression, McPherson was one of the few areas of the country that avoided the downturn. The refinery and the wheat fields continued to thrive. Jobs were plentiful, and families had money to spend on luxuries such as basketball tickets. Reserved seats on the floor were seventy-five cents; general admission tickets in the balcony, forty.

Game nights were a blast, with Augie San Romani's twenty-five-piece band entertaining the crowd with the latest tunes. Afterward, fans gathered at the Oke Doke Inn for barbecue or at Sam's 81 Café for a coffee. When the Refiners played big games out of town, San Romani's band and hundreds of fans loaded onto a train to join them. Fans who couldn't make the trip crowded around the offices of the *Daily Republican* newspaper on South Main, listening to updates relayed by a Western Union telegraph operator seated courtside.

Coach Johnson valued tall players like Schmidt. In those days, there was a jump ball at center court after every made basket. A team with a tall center could score, win the jump ball, keep possession, and score again. And tall players collected rebounds off their teammates' missed shots. Francis Johnson (the coach's ambidextrous younger brother), Tex Gibbons, Jack Ragland, and Bill Wheatley would heave up shots mainly for the chance for one of the big guys—Schmidt and six-foot-eight teammate Joe Fortenberry—to grab a rebound and putback. They cared little about shooting percentages.

This was a legitimate strategy some teams still use today, with guards driving to the basket and big men crashing the boards. Johnson was an innovator in other ways, too, always collecting new ideas, looking for a competitive edge. He once took a team to Mexico for a series of exhibition games. The Mexican teams were severely overmatched, but Johnson learned a valuable lesson. On defense, the Mexican players all chased the ball the way kids do when they're learning to play soccer—one big scrum surrounding the ball from baseline to baseline. Johnson was intrigued. What if he incorporated more strategy into such a swarming defense? He developed a 2–2–1 pressing defense, two men on the ball at all times, and it worked wonders. Well into the 1980s, there were college coaches running the same defense who remembered it originated with Johnson. With his pressure defense and fast-break offense, Johnson called his style of hoops "Fire Department Basketball," best played at breakneck speed, like an engine screeching its way to a blaze. In an era when coaches and fans were accustomed to a much slower pace of play, some critics called it bad basketball.

That may be true, Johnson would allow, but his boys "could play bad basketball better than anybody else."

*Coach Gene Johnson and the Globe Refiners basketball team were the biggest thing to hit McPherson, Kansas, since the discovery of oil. A colorful promoter, Johnson decked his team out in new uniforms and attracted overflow crowds to home games.* (McPherson Museum)

*Bill Wheatley didn't make his college basketball team, but he was one of the stars of the Globe Refiners and the U.S. Olympic team. Later in life, he traveled the world teaching the game to children as part of a U.S. State Department program.* (McPherson Museum)

# CHAPTER ELEVEN

# Big Time

The 1936 U.S. Olympic basketball tryouts were structured much differently than they are today. Players wouldn't try out as individuals. Rather, eight amateur teams would come to New York City for a qualifying tournament in early April, and whichever two teams advanced to the championship game would be combined to create the Olympic team. Succeeding as a team was what mattered.

Ever the innovative coach, Gene Johnson took the Refiners to New York three weeks early for an exhibition game against a team of area college All-Stars. Wanting his players to have an advantage when it came time for the Olympic qualifying tournament, he brought his team to New York ahead of schedule to get used to playing at Madison Square Garden, to visit the city's tourist sites so the players could concentrate on basketball the next time around, and, equally important for a showman like Johnson, to generate lots of publicity.

Johnson understood one thing about New Yorkers: if there's something in their city they like, they'll say it's the very best. Anywhere. And if they've never seen something before, they'll claim it's never been done. Anywhere.

So, when sportswriter Arthur Daley of the *New York Times* watched the Globe Refiners practice at New York's West Side YMCA before the game against the college All-Stars, witnessing things he'd never seen, he was flabbergasted.

He marveled at the Refiners' pressure defense. "No team around here ever played at such breathless pace and with such furious drive," he wrote. "They never stop digging."

And he was shocked by the unusual way big men like Willard Schmidt and Joe Fortenberry shot their layups, compelled to describe their revolutionary style in terms he suspected his readers would understand.

"They left the floor, reached up and pitched the ball downward into the hoop, much like a cafeteria customer dunking a roll in coffee."

Arthur Daley had just described the first slam dunks he'd ever witnessed to people who'd never seen one before, either. In the days before ESPN and social media, it was a big deal for these players to capture the attention of the New York sportswriters. These newspapermen were the builders of legends, and Joe Fortenberry, the All-American from West Texas who, according to Daley, was the first man ever to dunk a basketball, had all the makings of a legend.

They say everything's bigger in Texas, and Fortenberry proved the point from

WILLARD SCHMIDT — 6 FEET 9 INCHES TALL !!

I'LL DUNK IT TO MAKE SURE.

TALK ABOUT SKY-SCRAPERS !!

JOE FORTENBERRY THE OILERS' 6-FOOT 8-INCH ALL-AMERICA CENTER !!

GENE JOHNSON — CLEVER COACH OF THE MCPHERSON (KAS.) GLOBE REFINERS - NATIONAL A.A.U. BASKETBALL CHAMPIONS

*A cartoon in* Amateur Athlete *magazine marveled at the height of the Globe Refiners.* (McPherson Museum)

the very beginning. He was born big as a Longhorn bull, tipping the scales at thirteen pounds, fourteen ounces. By the age of eleven, he was six feet tall. As a boy, Joe needed all the strength that came with his giant frame. From the age of eight, he worked the family farm, cultivating the soil with a horse-drawn plow, picking cotton by hand, wrangling cattle. No electricity, no heavy machinery, plenty of hot sun and dirt and dust in the Texas panhandle. He learned to play basketball shooting at a hoop nailed to the side of a barn.

Joe was a gentle giant, never a bully, a protective type who never uttered a cross word. But his strength and athleticism were legendary. In an era when every small town in the area claimed a bare-knuckle boxing champ, Joe Fortenberry was the pride of Happy, Texas. Nothing illustrated Fortenberry's strong-but-steady demeanor as a legend of West Texas more than one very brief boxing match.

A cocky fighter from Clayton, New Mexico, challenged eighteen-year-old Fortenberry to a bout, driving 150 desolate miles to Happy for the occasion. After sundown, spectators arranged their cars in a circle, pointing their headlights toward a dry lake bed. The challenger whooped and hollered, boasting about the pain he'd inflict on Fortenberry. Joe was nowhere to be found. Was he scared? Finally, off in the distance, the rumble of an approaching car. It was Fortenberry, driving solo. Before Joe could get out of his car, the fighter from Clayton rushed up and pulled a cheap shot, sucker punching Fortenberry in the driver's seat. Still seated, Joe punched back hard with his left hand, knocking the punk out cold. He started up his car and drove home, winning the fight without ever leaving his seat or speaking a word.

Initially, everything worked out on this first New York trip just as Coach Johnson hoped. Cocky and outspoken as usual, he was a hit with the sportswriters, boasting that his team wasn't only the tallest in the country, but the best, too. "The tall tales of tall men were told by a short visitor," wrote John Kieran of the *New York Times*, describing the coach as a "lively gent with a strong voice, curly brown hair, genial grin and rimless spectacles." If his team couldn't beat a bunch of college players, Johnson claimed, he wasn't much of a coach.

He almost had to eat his words. The Refiners got off to an awful offensive start against the college All-Stars, making just six of forty-two shots in the first half. But in what Daley described as "the most brilliantly played and spectacular basketball game that Madison Square Garden ever has seen," the Refiners made a dramatic comeback, squeaking past the All-Stars 45–43. It turned out Johnson had been wise to schedule this practice game. The reason his players had such a hard time making baskets? They had never played on a court with glass backboards and found the Garden's clear boards, designed so fans sitting behind them could see through, disorienting. Down by ten points in the second half, the "fire wagon attack" finally got into high gear. Though the Garden fans were up and out of their seats, screaming their heads off in support of the faltering hometown collegians, Fortenberry and Francis Johnson led a furious fourth-quarter rally, and the Refiners were victorious.

After the game, the coach of the All-Stars, Clair Bee of powerhouse Long Island University, praised the Refiners' unorthodox style and predicted they had a strong chance to win the Olympic qualifying tournament. "They play crazy basketball," he said. "I have to admit it takes a real team to keep up with them."

Everyone expected the Refiners to win the qualifying tournament three weeks later.

But sports can be full of surprises.

# CHAPTER TWELVE

# Choices

The Olympic qualifying tournament was supposed to be the biggest event in the history of basketball, and the venue was fitting for the occasion.

Madison Square Garden was loud, colorful, and exciting, the center of the sports universe in 1936, the place where everyone from neighborhood gamblers to New York's rich and famous converged to watch top boxing matches, basketball doubleheaders, and even professional hockey. But for Refiner Bill Wheatley of tiny Gypsum, Kansas, the Garden might as well have been the world's largest barn.

"Jesus!" he exclaimed as he gazed around the huge arena. "How many bales of hay would this place hold?"

Promoter Ned Irish had promised sellout crowds, and U.S. Olympic officials counted on ticket sales from these games, as well as the earlier rounds played at other sites, not only to bankroll the basketball team's trip to Germany but also to pay most of the expenses for the rest of the nearly four hundred Olympians.

One of the biggest advertisers in the tournament's printed program was the German national railway line, an arm of Joseph Goebbels's propaganda machine posing as a tourist bureau. But the Nazis didn't get their money's worth. Only five thousand people bothered to show up for the championship game, and at least one thousand of them were college coaches in town for a convention. Ticket sales wouldn't even pay the expenses for the winning basketball teams to get on the boat to Germany.

Eight teams arrived in New York for the Olympic qualifier, including the Refiners and Universals, the culmination of a national tournament open to teams from the AAU, NCAA, and YMCA. The NCAA tournament didn't exist yet, and there was no precedent for a national postseason tournament for the colleges. Many chose not to participate. Some cited budget concerns, others didn't want their players to miss more class time, and some in the South feared conflicts with spring football practice.

For the players at Long Island University, the choice was more profound. As they debated whether to play, they considered questions of morality. Could they in good conscience compete for the U.S. team if that implied an endorsement of the Nazi regime? Even if they didn't win the tournament, merely playing in it—and attracting thousands of hometown fans to the Garden—would help raise funds for the U.S. Olympic team's participation in Germany. The moral high ground can be easy to take when there's really nothing at stake to begin with. But for LIU, a decision to boycott the tournament would come at great personal sacrifice. The Blackbirds were 25–0 and in the midst of an overall forty-three-game winning streak. Many considered them the best college team in the country. Even facing top AAU teams, they would be legitimate contenders to win the qualifying tournament.

Blackbird head coach Clair Bee gathered his seven players and made the terms clear: one vote to boycott would keep the team out of the tournament. If just one player opposed playing in Hitler's Germany, that was enough for him. Some of his players were Jewish, some weren't. But they were one team. Four hands went up in support of the boycott; all players left the locker room unanimous in the decision. These were their names: Leo Merson. Ben Kramer. Jules Bender. Marius Russo. Art Hillhouse. William Schwartz. Ken Norton.

While the Long Island players chose a principled stand, another team chose the opposite approach, attempting to cheat its way into the tournament.

A team representing the Denver YMCA won the national Y tournament and the right to come to New York but was disqualified at the last minute when officials discovered something fishy. The players looked familiar. In fact, the same players had competed in the national AAU tournament under a different name, the Denver Safeways. With the Denver Y disqualified, the runner-up team from the Wilmerding (Pennsylvania) YMCA earned a last-minute invitation to the tournament. Arkansas, Washington, Utah State, DePaul, and Temple represented the colleges, and the AAU's top two teams, the Refiners and Universals, rounded out the field of eight. While McPherson arrived full of confidence after having beaten the Universals in the AAU championship game in Denver a week earlier, the boys from Los Angeles were in complete disarray.

The movie studio itself was in such deep financial straits that Carl Laemmle, its founder, was forced to sell the company only a day before the New York tournament began. Jack Pierce, the makeup artist who'd founded the team, couldn't accompany the team to the most important tournament it had ever played, called back to Hollywood in the midst of the sale. Guard Lloyd Goldstein made the trip but quit playing after the team's first game against Arkansas, and various excuses were given for the player's sudden absence. Some reports said he was sick. Others said he had been disqualified for having received $10 to play in a baseball game, jeopardizing the amateur status then required to compete in the Olympics. Still others claimed that as a Jewish person, Goldstein decided to quit playing in protest of Hitler, insinuating that the studio bosses had convinced him to make that decision. In this theory, there may have been truth. Prior to the New York tournament, Laemmle and Universal had dropped their support of the team in protest of the Hitler regime.

All told, the Universals arrived in the Big Apple without their founder or their sponsor, with their employer up for sale, a coach they resented, no guarantee of jobs when they returned, and short one player.

To the modern eye, something else was conspicuously absent from the proceedings in New York: African American players. Every team competing in the tournament, including the Refiners and Universals, was all-white, evidence of the separate and unequal status of American basketball at the time. AAU teams hadn't integrated yet (in part reflecting the racist hiring practices of the companies that sponsored them), and black people played for segregated YMCA teams, none of which were invited to the tournament. Only a handful of predominantly white colleges had desegregated their programs. (At the University of Kansas, for example, Phog Allen wouldn't recruit his first black player until 1951. In 1936, African American student John McLendon couldn't play for Allen and the Jayhawks, but he watched the team's practices and soaked up every bit of basketball knowledge he could from his favorite physical education professor, James Naismith. Naismith befriended and mentored McLendon, who went on to become a highly successful collegiate and professional head coach and was inducted into the Naismith Basketball Hall of Fame.)

THE HOWARD UNIVERSITY VARSITY BASKETBALL TEAM FOR 1926

*While the 1936 U.S. Olympic basketball team was all-white, it wasn't because African Americans didn't play basketball or weren't good enough to make the team; it was because of racism that restricted opportunities for black players. Here's the Howard University team of 1926. (New York Public Library)*

Many of the best African American basketball players in the 1930s played professionally for barnstorming teams such as the Harlem Globetrotters and New York Renaissance and therefore, as nonamateurs, were ineligible for the Olympics under the rules of the era. Not that it would have mattered. While white Olympic officials were okay with a few black stars competing in individual sports such as track and boxing, there was great resistance to a black presence in team sports. Giving a black team the opportunity to compete in the trials with the chance to make up half of the entire U.S. basketball team was an unthinkable proposition to the white men in charge. In fact, when UCLA's Don Barksdale became the first African American Olympic basketball player at the 1948 Games in London, it came only after strenuous objections from some coaches and Olympic officials. Even after Barksdale broke the color line, for decades only a token number of black players were allowed to earn spots on the U.S. basketball team. It wasn't until the 1976 Games in Montreal that Team USA had more black players than white.

In their whites-only structure in 1936, U.S. amateur basketball and the Olympic basketball tryout system were hardly different from the policies in Germany that prevented Jewish athletes from joining athletic clubs or competing for Olympic teams.

But while black people were shut out of the basketball tryouts, the irony of the Nazis adding basketball to the Olympics and the U.S. holding its qualifying tournament in New York was that Jewish people in the city played a prominent role at the sport's highest levels, including their tremendous influence at Madison Square Garden as both spectators and players.

The Garden was the mecca of college basketball in the 1930s because of the wildly successful college doubleheaders staged there, with top teams traveling to the Big Apple to play local powerhouses such as City College of New York, New York University, and Long Island University—all schools with rosters full of Jewish players. These marquee games matching Jewish stars against the country's best competition attracted so much attention they transformed college basketball from a sport with scattered regional followings to one with a national rooting interest. Fans learned the names of top players from Kentucky to California, followed their exploits in the newspapers, and—in these days before television— yearned to see them play in person.

Basketball wasn't just a popular spectator sport, but an important part of Jewish youth culture in New York, with kids learning the game at immigrant settlement houses, playgrounds, and schools. These pickup games led to more formal contests in the Public School Athletic League—an organization launched by none other than James Naismith's former mentor in Springfield, Luther Gulick, yet another manifestation of Gulick's desire to introduce play and games into the lives of young people.

Jewish prominence in basketball, in New York and elsewhere, even led to the creation of prejudiced stereotypes. When the Refiners traveled east, they were aware of what was dubbed "East Coast Jew Ball," a brand of hoops marked by constant motion, rapid passing, and sharp cuts to the basket. Paul Gallico of the *New York Daily News* dredged up several anti-Semitic stereotypes in explaining away Jewish basketball excellence, claiming the sport appealed to Jewish people because "the game places a premium on an alert, scheming mind and flashy trickiness, artful dodging and general smartalecness."

Regardless, even as the image of a solitary farm boy shooting at a hoop affixed to the side of a barn in Indiana, Kentucky, or Kansas took hold in the American consciousness, so, too, did the image of basketball as a city game, an avenue for hardscrabble kids to make good. Madison Square Garden was where these threads first converged.

As expected, the Universals, despite all the upheaval within their team and at their employer's, made their way to the title game, easily beating the University of Arkansas (40–29) and the Wilmerding YMCA (42–29), while the Refiners escaped with a close win over Temple University (56–48) and crushed the University of Washington (48–30).

Since both the Universals and Refiners had earned the right to place players on the Olympic team by advancing this far, the championship game was anticlimactic, and that may have partly explained the small crowd. Plus, there was no local team competing, and because New York City had been the center of the U.S. boycott movement, some fans may have stayed away on principle.

In the title game, the Refiners played less like a fire department and more like a lifeless fire log. No zip, no dash, no enthusiasm. And no accuracy, either; the Refiners shot the ball ninety times and made only sixteen baskets. Vernon Vaughn fouled out in the first half, and Francis Johnson joined him on the bench just five minutes into the second half. With the Globe Refiners missing two starters, Carl Shy and Carl Knowles led the way for the Universals, scoring twelve points apiece.

Lubin added eleven, and when the final buzzer sounded, the Universals had pulled off the upset, winning 44–43.

*Madison Square Garden in New York City was the center of the basketball universe in the 1930s. In April 1936, the Universals of Hollywood (in white) beat the Globe Refiners of McPherson, Kansas, to win the Olympic qualifying tournament.* (McPherson Museum)

In years to come, Refiners coach Gene Johnson explained the surprising loss by claiming that he had agreed to a request by Needles to take it easy on the Universals, to let up on defense and not pressure the ball. Given Johnson's competitiveness and the fact that the winner of the game earned the right to place one more player on the Olympic team than the loser, that explanation is hard to buy. Some, including Johnson's descendants, have hinted that the "fix was in," with gamblers having influenced referee Ernie Quigley to call the game in the underdog

THIS CERTIFIES THAT

## William Wheatley

WON 2nd PLACE IN THE Basketball Event
IN THE FINAL TRY OUTS AT New York, 4-5-36
HELD BY THE AMERICAN OLYMPIC COMMITTEE
TO SELECT A TEAM TO REPRESENT THE UNITED
STATES OF AMERICA AT THE GAMES OF THE
XI OLYMPIAD, BERLIN, GERMANY, 1936.

*Frederick W. Rubien*
SECRETARY

*Avery Brundage*
PRESIDENT

*Here's the second-place certificate Bill Wheatley received from the American Olympic Committee after the Refiners lost to the Universals in the qualifying tournament. Second place was good enough to make the Olympic team, however.* (McPherson Museum)

Universals' favor. Others claim that Quigley despised Coach Johnson and intentionally called fouls on Francis Johnson and Vaughn so they'd foul out. There's no evidence to support these claims.

Whatever the reason, the game, while exciting in its final minutes, had not delivered on its promise, and the same could be said for the entire tournament. The composition of the Olympic team had been determined, the Refiners and Universals merged to create USA Basketball's first-ever "Dream Team," but there had been no special magic to the proceedings nor the sellout crowds that had been predicted. Walking off the court, reporters peppered Sam Balter with questions that had more to do with international politics than hoops. Since basketball held its Olympic qualifying event before other sports, Balter, if he chose to accept the roster spot, would officially become the first Jewish member of the U.S. Olympic team.

Like it or not, he had a big decision to make.

*Members of the Universal Pictures basketball team pose immediately after beating the Globe Refiners at the 1936 U.S. qualifying tournament at Madison Square Garden. Sam Balter, on the far left, had an important decision to make. As a Jewish person, would he accept a spot on the U.S. team and travel to Nazi Germany?* (Getty Images)

# CHAPTER THIRTEEN

# On Their Own

Sam Balter's parents, Samuel and Sofie, had escaped the anti-Semites by hiding under a bale of hay, slipping past Russian border guards in a horse-drawn carriage around the turn of the twentieth century.

Making their way to London, broke, Samuel sold baked potatoes on street corners; Sofie sewed for neighbors. The teenagers earned enough money for one ticket to America. Samuel sailed first, found work as a locksmith, and saved enough money in six months to send for his bride. An immigration society provided free train tickets to Detroit. Samuel went to work at the Ford factory. He and Sofie started a family (their third son, Sam, was born in 1909), saved their money, and moved to California. These immigrants were living the American Dream, and they created it for others, too. Samuel built nice houses in Southern California, always with saunas inside, sometimes indoor pools, too.

As Jewish people and gentiles and newspapermen and community leaders questioned his commitment to his faith or his country in 1936, Sammy Balter already knew all about anti-Semitism—in his parents' case, in Belarus rather than Germany—and how it could tear families apart. But he needed look no further than to his mom and dad to see examples of incredible courage, resistance, and triumph in the face of religious hatred.

Religious liberty in America meant the freedom to practice his faith however Sammy Balter saw fit, and for him that meant cultural Judaism more than religious observance. As a kid, he never attended synagogue. When he turned thirteen, there was no bar mitzvah. He thought religion was fine for those who wanted it, but he believed many crimes had been committed in its name. He was skeptical of the fanaticism it bred. His daughter later wrote that he "stood for humanity and not ideology." In any event, he was his own man. He would listen to the opinions of others, but no one could tell him what to do.

Not that they didn't try.

Some Jewish people said he'd be a traitor to the faith if he participated in the Olympics. Other friends said sports and politics should be kept separate, and he might as well go. Some said he'd never find work in Hollywood again if he played, since the major studios were run by Jewish people. Balter did more than just listen; he sought out the opinions of those he respected, especially within the

Jewish community. But those voices began to turn him off, he said later, when they became too personal and judgmental, "reduced from any high-minded debate to a bitter individual rebuke."

In the end, he said, he decided to go to Germany because, "all in all, it seemed the proper thing to do." He loved playing basketball, and maybe he was rationalizing, he admitted, but it seemed the best course was to go to the Olympics, play well, and disprove the notion that Jewish people were inferior beings. All men, he believed, were created equal.

Questions of morality and politics aside, the most pressing concern for Balter and his teammates after returning home to Los Angeles after the qualifying tournament was to scrape together enough money to get back to New York before the SS *Manhattan* sailed to Germany. With Universal's sponsorship kaput and no funds coming from the American Olympic Committee, Balter and his teammates needed to raise their own money for train tickets back to New York. In McPherson, Globe Oil told Gene Johnson and the Refiners that they were on their own, too. There were no guarantees that jobs would be waiting for them after the Olympics, either, and newspaper reports suggested that Globe planned to drop its AAU sponsorship after the summer Games. These were especially troubling developments for one member of the team. With a wife and new baby to support, center Vernon Vaughn decided he couldn't take a chance on losing his job at the refinery. He had earned the right to compete in the Olympics but gave up his spot. Willard Schmidt had expected to be left behind in McPherson, but now he inherited Vaughn's place.

## Universal Pictures National Championship Basket Ball Team

*James Needles, coach; Carl Shy, Don Piper, Frank Lubin, Lloyd Goldstein, Carl Knowles, Duane Swanson, Art Mollner, Sam Balder, Carl Marias, trainer, Jack Pierce, manager.*

## CHARLES R. ROGERS TAKES CHARGE OF PRODUCTION AT UNIVERSAL CITY

CHARLES R. ROGERS, Executive Vice President of Universal Pictures and in charge of all production at Universal City, in his first public statement, announced that Universal would c... present...

pansion of department demands. During the past two weeks 11 new

**CONVENTION MAY 25**

The story conf... es at Universal City are ... The line for...

writers have been added to the scenario staff presided over by Jerry Sackheim, and four directors, namely, Ralph Murphy, Walter Lang, Edward Buzzell and Arthur Lubin have been...

*After beating the Refiners at Madison Square Garden in the Olympic qualifying tournament, the Universals basketball team was featured in the studio's weekly newsletter.* (Universal Studios Licensing LLC)

In Los Angeles, Braven Dyer, the same *LA Times* sports editor who had arranged for Jimmy Needles to coach the Universals, organized a game against area college players to raise the $2,000 (about $35,000 today) necessary to get the Olympians to New York. But attendance at the game was light, and the team collected only $500. Just as embarrassing, the collegians, playing together for the first time, won the game. Newspaper reporters joked that maybe the wrong team was headed to the Olympics.

Jokes aside, there was now a serious chance the Universals wouldn't make the trip to Germany because they couldn't afford train tickets to New York. Reports circulated around the country that the team wasn't going to make it to the *Manhattan*. The Refiners held out some hope they'd be the only team going to the Olympics, which would mean more playing time for all of them. Fortunately for the Universals, the team's prior association with the movie studio had its advantages. Several Hollywood stars pitched in with last-minute donations, including animator and the director of *Frankenstein* Walter Lantz, who would go on to invent the cartoon character Woody Woodpecker. "The local boys, who had given up all hope of making the trip, were so happy at the unexpected turn of events that they could barely talk," one local newspaper reported. "They barely had time to make the train after extending heartfelt gratitude to those who made their trip possible."

With no wealthy celebrities to call on for money in McPherson, Gene Johnson visited Main Street merchants door to door, and players sold fans Dollar Donation Fund tickets, all with a goal of raising $1,000 for the trip to New York. "A small donation from everybody will do it," Johnson said, "and nobody will miss the money." Ever the proud showman, Johnson greatly resented the fact he was put in such a position by the American Olympic Committee. Even as his players practiced daily in the heat of a scorching Midwest summer, they practically begged their neighbors for dollar bills. But Johnson realized there was no other option. "It's a shame that our Olympic team is handled in such a manner that a team, the best in the nation, having won the right to go should have to

GLORIA STUART  CHESTER MORRIS  CARL LAEMMLE  MARGARET SULLAVAN  BUCK JONES

JOIN M. STAHL

UNIVERSAL PICTURES

BASKETBALL

JACK P. PIERCE, MANAGER

ALL-STARS

CHARLIE "CHUCK" HYATT, CAPTAIN

KARLOFF

ROGER PRYOR    BINNIE BARNES    CARL LAEMMLE, JR.  JAMES WHALE    HENRY HULL

*Members of the 1935 Universals team pose with a banner featuring the names of their sponsors. James Whale was the director of* Frankenstein *and Boris Karloff was the actor who portrayed the monster. And see the cartoon character in the bottom corners? That's not Mickey Mouse, but a character a young animator named Walt Disney created before he came up with Mickey. His name was Oswald the Rabbit.* (Los Angeles Public Library)

help finance themselves," he said. "But when it simmers down to help or stay home I think we should help these boys who have played so hard and well for McPherson."

Dollar by dollar, the funds came in from the men, women, and children of McPherson. There would be enough money for gas, food, and lodging to pack the six players and three family members into two cars for the long drive to New York.

But as soon as one crisis was averted, two more popped up in its place.

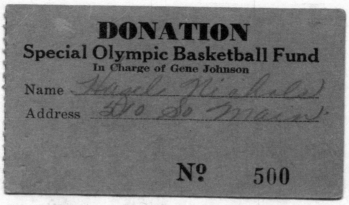

*When the McPherson Refiners qualified for the Olympics, they still had to raise enough money to pay for their trip from Kansas to New York to board the SS* Manhattan. *Hazel Nichols was one of the McPherson fans who purchased a $1 donation ticket to support the team.* (McPherson Museum)

Showering at the refinery, Willard Schmidt stepped barefoot on a piece of tin, slicing his foot so badly it required eight stitches. He'd spend the next few weeks walking around in a pair of comfortable slippers, eventually pulling the stitches out himself on board the *Manhattan.*

At least Schmidt didn't nearly kill himself. That distinction belonged to his teammates Joe Fortenberry and Tex Gibbons. On the sweltering night of July 3, two local boosters invited Fortenberry and Gibbons to join them on a joyride down Highway 81 in a brand-new Chevrolet. Newspapers later reported there might have been some drinking involved, while the players claimed a large truck forced them off the road. Whatever the cause, the '36 Chevy went careening off the highway, tumbling over several times before coming to a stop in a ditch. Gibbons suffered a six-inch gash along his right forearm and nearly had his right ear torn off. Fortenberry, the bare-knuckle boxer, walked away with bruises to his head.

For Coach Johnson, the signals were clear: it was time to get his boys on the boat to Germany before anybody else got hurt.

*The Globe Refiners packed into cars like this one for their long drive between Kansas and New York. Here they stop for gas on the way back from New York.* (McPherson Museum)

# CHAPTER FOURTEEN

# You Can't Beat Fun

After a brutally hot, slow, and cramped 1,400-mile automobile drive from McPherson, the Globe Refiners finally emerged from New York's Holland Tunnel into Manhattan late in the evening of July 12. They drove up Broadway to see the famous lights of Times Square, then checked into the Lincoln Hotel and fell fast asleep.

The next morning, five of the players took a subway to the Bronx to watch the New York Yankees play the Chicago White Sox. They were thrilled to see a rookie named Joe DiMaggio patrol the outfield and slugger Lou Gehrig (three years away from his ALS diagnosis) blast a home run. That night, they were fitted for the shoes and hat they'd wear in the opening ceremonies (size 15C shoes and a 7 ⅛ hat for Willard Schmidt).

The next night, the gang took an hour-long subway ride out to Coney Island, the world's largest amusement park. Schmidt wrote a letter to his wife, Hazel, declaring he'd never had so much fun in his life, staying out until two a.m. and spending what little money he had "right and left like it was water." He rode the gigantic Cyclone wooden roller coaster five times, looped around on a hundred-foot-high Ferris wheel, splashed down a water slide, and banged around with his teammates in bumper cars "until I thought we would bust. I guess you can't beat fun."

*Before they boarded the SS* Manhattan *for the voyage to Germany, members of the U.S. basketball team enjoyed the attractions at New York's Coney Island, the country's largest amusement park.* (New York Public Library)

The fun didn't stop aboard ship.

If eating on the SS *Manhattan* had been an Olympic sport, there could have been a three-hundred-way tie for the gold medal. Schmidt recalled that eating—and not just eating, but eating frequently; and not just eating frequently, but eating copious amounts of delicious food, frequently—so quickly became part of the shipboard routine that he was seated in the dining room devouring his first meal when he realized the *Manhattan* hadn't even passed the Statue of Liberty yet.

Who could blame him? Surviving the hardships of the Great Depression was reason enough to take advantage of the endless supply of food. Schmidt, a string bean at six foot nine, two hundred pounds, was getting enough to eat for the first time in his life.

*Every member of the U.S. Olympic delegation received a passenger list like this one on board the SS Manhattan. Bill Wheatley saved his and his family eventually donated it to the McPherson Museum in Kansas. (McPherson Museum)*

More than enough.

Take, for example, this dinner menu that lay before him and the other American athletes on July 20.

### Hors d'oeuvres:
dill pickles, tomato juice cocktail, spiced pears, grapefruit, salad, herring with onions, green olives, pickled walnuts

### Soups:
essence of tomatoes, jellied beef broth

### Fish:
boiled pickerel

### Entrees:
chicken liver sauté, risotto à la créole, veal, fried calf's head with tomato sauce

### Roasts:
prime rib, milk-fed chicken

### From the Grill:
sausage, rump steak with A1 sauce

### Veggies:
green peas and asparagus tips, buttered white squash

### Potatoes:
boiled, baked, mashed, or French fried

### Salads:
tomato, romaine, with French, Russian, or Nanking dressing

### Dessert:
baba au chocolat, strawberry water ice, French apple cake, coffee ice cream, assorted cookies,

### Fresh fruit basket, Tea, Coffee, Milk

### Cheese:
cream, American, Stilton, Cheshire, Swiss with crackers or pretzels

And this was just one dinner, capping off a day at sea that had already included early morning pastries, breakfast, coffee break, lunch, and tea service. After dinner, athletes roamed the ship looking for late-night snacks when they weren't "souvenir collecting," as track star Louis Zamperini put it, snatching up everything from towels to ashtrays as mementoes of the trip.

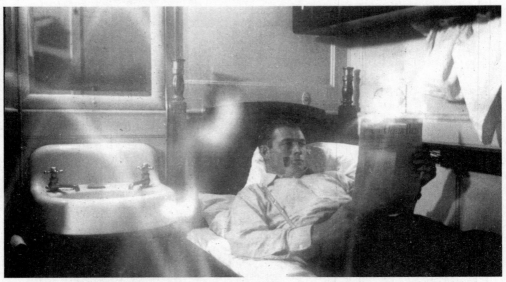

*American basketball player Bill Wheatley reads a newspaper while puffing on a pipe in his stateroom aboard the SS* Roosevelt *on his return from the Olympics. Living conditions on the trip to Germany aboard the SS* Manhattan *were similar.* (McPherson Museum)

In addition to all the food, there was entertainment galore. Schmidt enjoyed playing shuffleboard, tennis, Ping-Pong, and checkers during the day, and each night after dinner there was a talent or variety show, including a Monte Carlo casino night where each athlete received pretend money.

But even without an opportunity to practice and with all the fun diversions, the basketball players began to appreciate the significance of this trip. First came

*American basketball giants Joe Fortenberry and Willard Schmidt enjoy a game of shuffleboard aboard the SS* Manhattan. *When they weren't eating, the American Olympians enjoyed a variety of amusements.* (McPherson Museum)

the team picture, everyone lining up in their red, white, and blue uniforms in two neat rows. Then their blue jackets and white flannel slacks for the opening ceremonies appeared in their cabins along with a minute-by-minute schedule of events for the ceremonies. Schmidt and teammate Francis Johnson were fortunate. Assigned to Room 54 on Deck D, they were the only basketball players with an ocean view from their bunks. Occasionally, they'd open their porthole for a breath of cool air, only to slam the window shut when salty sea water sprayed in. Now they kept the window closed so their Olympic uniforms wouldn't be ruined. Everything seemed real and immediate. This was actually happening.

Sam Balter, the guard from Los Angeles, began to feel uneasy. This wasn't seasickness. Ever since his Universals won the Olympic tryouts at Madison Square Garden and he officially became the first Jewish member of the entire U.S. Olympic team, he had convinced himself that attending the Olympics, showing Hitler what a Jewish athlete could do, was the right decision. But now he was

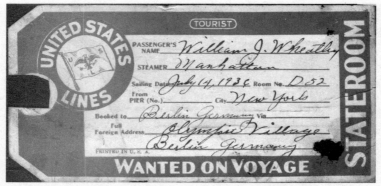

*Bill Wheatley's stateroom tag specified he was bound for the Olympic Village in Berlin, Germany, and listed his room number aboard the SS* Manhattan. *(McPherson Museum)*

hearing anti-Semitic comments from American Olympic officials that made him uncomfortable.

The SS *Manhattan* barreled on toward Germany, and there was no turning back.

While everyone around him had carefree fun, Sam Balter wondered whether he'd made a huge mistake.

*Members of the first-ever U.S. Olympic basketball team pose in full uniform aboard the SS* Manhattan *on the way to Germany. They would lose several basketballs to the Atlantic Ocean when practicing on deck. (McPherson Museum)*

# CHAPTER FIFTEEN

# Welcome to Germany

A t first, just a few Americans on the deck of the SS *Manhattan* saw it; then more athletes rushed up to the rails to take a look.

On shore, German men and women danced and sang under a canopy of electric lights strung from tree to tree, raising their beer steins in a salute to the Olympians as they drifted slowly by. Water polo player Herb Wildman remembered this scene for decades, calling it one of the "most glorious sights" of his life.

The SS *Manhattan* had reached Germany around eleven thirty p.m. on July 23, making its way down the Elbe River to Hamburg, where the athletes would sleep on board so they could disembark first thing in the morning for a series of welcoming ceremonies there and in Berlin.

Lights on the SS *Manhattan* illuminated the U.S. and Olympic flags; there was no mistaking who was aboard this ship. Germans by the riverside shouted greetings to the Americans, who removed their caps and waved back. Small boats blinked their lights and sounded their whistles and horns.

As the American athletes returned to their cabins and settled into their bunks for one final sleep aboard the SS *Manhattan*, they replayed these images in their heads. If first impressions meant anything, it appeared they would have a great time in Nazi Germany.

Five a.m. came early the next morning, with 334 young athletes waking up, yawning, stretching, eating a quick breakfast, and gathering their belongings after nine days at sea. As they disembarked at a rain-soaked Hamburg pier at exactly six a.m., the Americans heard the exotic rumble of hundreds of German voices

*American Olympic team members step off the SS* Manhattan *in Hamburg, Germany, welcomed by the swastika, symbol of the evil Nazi regime.* (U.S. Holocaust Memorial Museum, courtesy of National Archives)

up ahead in a reception hall, and they recognized the familiar patriotic American marching tunes of John Philip Sousa played by a German band. And the first thing they saw? A large banner draped over the entrance to the hall reading WELCOME TO GERMANY. The sign was flanked on the right by the stars and stripes and on the left by the most evil symbol in the world, the new, official, red-white-and-black flag of Nazi Germany, the swastika.

After welcome speeches, the hosts passed out free cigars, wine, beer, and orange juice. The Americans boarded buses for a short ride to city hall. As he gazed out the window, Willard Schmidt noticed a strange and unnatural uniformity in everything he saw. Thousands of people lined the streets, and every single one of them raised their arms in the Hitler salute as the Americans drove by. Even the street sweepers behaved as one, sweeping together, as if synchronized street sweeping were an Olympic sport. At city hall, Schmidt and his teammates sipped champagne from delicate one-hundred-year-old glasses and pretended to listen to a series of short speeches most of them couldn't understand. Next, it was on to the railroad station, where the Americans would board the *Flying Hamburger*, named after the city of Hamburg, for a speedy (ninety-nine-mile-per-hour) ride to Berlin. As they gathered in the station, another German band bleated out military tunes. Spec Towns, a hurdler from Georgia, couldn't resist pulling a prank, grabbing the conductor's baton and leading everyone in song.

Turns out Towns's lark wasn't the only mischief the Americans got into on their first day in Germany. The *Flying Hamburger* hadn't even begun its trip to Berlin when German officials boarded the train and began searching the Americans' luggage. Several Olympians had taken the antique champagne glasses as souvenirs, continuing the pilfering that had begun on the *Manhattan*.

When the train arrived at the palatial Lehrter Bahnhof station in Berlin, the great Jesse Owens was startled. Even over the din of a brass band he could hear teenage girls shouting, *"Wo ist Jesse?! Wo ist Jesse?!"* (Where is Jesse?!) When Owens finally emerged from the train, he was besieged by German girls with scissors who began snipping off pieces of his suit. Luckily for Owens, he was literally the fastest man in the world, and he was able to scoot back onto the train, and to safety. Bill Wheatley had never seen such a mass of humanity. Fortenberry and Schmidt felt the gaze of thousands of eyes as people marveled at their height. They stood through more boring speeches, then were taken by bus to city hall for even more.

When Velma Dunn, a seventeen-year-old diver from Los Angeles, looked out her window at the throngs of Germans lining the streets, she was impressed with how many men she saw in military uniform. This was not something she was used to seeing in the United States. Piled into thirty buses with open tops, the Americans were treated to a tour of Berlin, through the Brandenburg Gate and the Tiergarten park and down the famous Unter den Linden boulevard, streets kept free of traffic by police. Even Sam Balter couldn't help but be impressed, with cheering fans crowding every sidewalk, window, balcony, and roof all along the journey. He found the scene warm and inspiring.

Finally, the buses arrived at the Olympic Village, a handsome new complex on the edge of a military base fifteen miles from downtown Berlin and nine miles from the cluster of sporting venues known as the Reichssportfeld. German soldiers

*German citizens raise their arms in the Nazi salute as they greet the U.S. Olympic team in the Berlin train station. Note the Nazi and Olympic flags hanging along the wall.* (U.S. Holocaust Memorial Museum, courtesy of National Archives)

in tall boots and swastikas greeted the team at the main entrance along with a military band and teen members of the Honorary Youth Service, dressed sharply in all white. After a flag-raising ceremony, the athletes received their identification badges and walked to their dormitories, a series of cream-colored stucco buildings with bright red Spanish tile roofs. Each lodge could sleep up to forty men (women stayed at their own quarters, the Friesenhaus, closer to the Olympic Stadium) and was named for a different village in Germany. The large track team occupied 105 (Bautzen), 106 (Chemnitz), and 107 (Plauen). Water polo and gymnastics checked into 95 (Gruben), while soccer and pistol shooting bunked in 93 (Potsdam). The basketball team took over lodge 101, named for the town of Dessau, once famous for its art and architecture school, the Bauhaus, which had been shut down by the Nazis.

Sam Balter had been disturbed by things he'd heard from American Olympic Committee president Avery Brundage ever since boarding the SS *Manhattan*. Brundage had addressed the U.S. athletes on deck, blasting opponents of American participation in the Games as misguided mischief makers out to thwart a noble cause. When the team toured Hamburg, Brundage referred glowingly to the Nazi hosts and criticized "disturbing forces" back home who threatened German-American friendship. To Balter, Brundage's comments sounded deferential to the Nazis and dismissive of the legitimate concerns of many Americans.

When Balter first arrived at the Olympic Village, he was taken aback by the heavy Nazi presence: men in shiny black boots and military uniforms emblazoned with swastikas, a nonstop barrage of Hitler salutes. The day was cold and overcast.

It felt more like November than July. The athletes were tired, their adrenaline plummeting after a busy morning of events tacked onto the end of a long sea voyage. After enduring weeks of record heat in the States, Balter's Olympic Village roommate Willard Schmidt relished the opportunity to grab some blankets and curl up in bed. Nothing like an afternoon nap on a gloomy day. While Schmidt slept, Balter relaxed in the common room in the Dessau suite, leafing through books and brochures left on a table. They were full of photos and propaganda promoting Hitler and his new Germany.

More than ever, Balter felt he had been misled by promises that these Games would be free of politics. It was clear Hitler was using the Olympics to sell Nazism.

*Accompanied by German soldiers, members of the U.S. Olympic team arrive at the Olympic Village. Sam Balter was bothered by the heavy Nazi presence at the Village. (U.S. Holocaust Memorial Museum, courtesy of Gerhard Vogel)*

# CHAPTER SIXTEEN

# The Anvil and the Hammer

H e was there, but nobody saw him.

Al Miller was used to sneaking around, avoiding attention. For a Jewish kid in Nazi Germany, it was partly a matter of survival, partly fun for a thirteen-year-old.

The consequences of getting caught weren't so dire on this summer day in 1936. It was just that visitors weren't allowed in the Olympic Village. But there he was, having the time of his life, watching athletes from all over the world in their colorful sweatshirts and uniforms.

Back in his neighborhood in the heart of Berlin's Wilmersdorf district, where Julius Streicher, publisher of the viciously anti-Semitic newspaper *Der Stürmer*, ranted against Jewish people at the Deutschlandhalle, Miller had learned how to

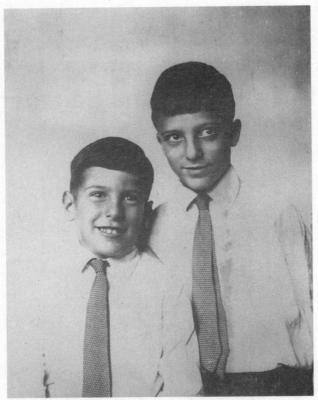

*As a young Jewish boy growing up in Berlin, Al Miller (left, with his brother) enjoyed playing soccer with his friends at school. When the Nazis came to power, however, Miller's former friends began to taunt him mercilessly. His parents sent him out of Germany for his safety, unsure if they'd ever see their son again.* (Al Miller)

slip around unnoticed, dodging streetcars and blending into the scenery to avoid trouble. He wasn't scared; he enjoyed the thrill, doing things he knew his parents wouldn't like. When he heard Nazi storm troopers marching through the streets, singing their hateful songs, he didn't run: he found a shadow, a place to hide in plain sight, so close to the thugs he could distinguish the lapel pins on their uniforms. When he couldn't hide quickly enough, he lifted his right arm in the Hitler salute. Trouble walked by.

As the last Jewish student remaining at his school, his goal was to fit in, even if it meant purposely missing a few questions on tests so he wouldn't stand out as the smartest. He shouted, *"Heil Hitler,"* and saluted every day along with his classmates. He played soccer with friends who wore swastikas on their Hitler Youth uniforms. He was just a kid who loved sports and school, trying to live a normal life.

At the dinner table, Miller's parents shared an outlook common to many Jewish Germans: *Hitler won't last. Jewish people have lived in Berlin since the thirteenth century and there have been troubles before. This will blow over. It can't get any worse.* Al's father was a patriotic German, had fought on the Russian Front in World War I. Al's grandfather had started a successful clothing business in Berlin, and his family still ran it. These were pillars of the community, contributors in so many ways.

But on the eve of the Olympics, even young Al could have told you how most Berliners looked at his family: like dirt.

As Sam Balter sat in the Olympic Village questioning his presence at these Games, daily life for the Miller family and the other hundreds of thousands of Jewish people in Germany was rapidly deteriorating. While the Nazis had not yet arrived at their "Final Solution" to murder all Jewish men, women, and children, their aim at this point was to eliminate any semblance of Jewish influence on German society, to make life miserable, to encourage emigration, and to confiscate Jewish property. Branding Jewish people as enemies of the state gave the Nazis a scapegoat for any and all problems and a rallying cry, unifying "Aryans" around their supposed superiority. The road to the Holocaust was paved with bullying, lies, propaganda, and a cynically calculated encouragement of intolerance.

This state-fueled anti-Semitism played out in individual acts of hatred every single day. Consider these examples, merely a handful of stories that illustrate how life had turned upside down for Jewish Germans, young and old, ordinary and prominent, even before the Olympics.

*Nazi propaganda minister Joseph Goebbels had no concern for telling the truth when influencing the German masses. In an interview with the* New York Times *in 1934, he cynically admitted as much. "The worth of propaganda cannot be judged by esthetic standards but only by reference to the results. Propaganda is a means to an end. If that end is attained, the means are good. Whether they satisfy exigent esthetic requirements is immaterial."* (U.S. Holocaust Memorial Museum, courtesy of National Archives)

Gerda Schild was fourteen at the time of the Olympics, living with her parents in the Bavarian town of Ansbach. Like Al Miller's, her father was a World War I veteran, a proud German, but that mattered little to her classmates and teachers. At recess, she and her friend Matilda were told to stand in the corner of the school-yard; anyone who dared play with them was punished. When she accompanied her parents to the market, she saw all the good stuff, like the Florida oranges, tucked beneath the counter so they couldn't buy it. On the radio, it was one Hitler speech after another, Jewish people blamed for everything wrong in the world. Neighbors hung banners proclaiming JEWS ARE OUR MISFORTUNE, and brown-shirted storm troopers—just ordinary young men she knew from town—marched at night by torchlight, singing lustfully of the violence they'd inflict on Jewish people. In the winter, kids who had been her friends pelted her with stones packed in ice and snow. There was nothing she could do to retaliate. "When they had their little Hitlerjugend [Hitler Youth] uniforms on, they felt like they were God themselves," she recalled.

The message she received—from teachers, from classmates, from the newspapers, from the leader of her country—was that she was stupid and nonhuman, unworthy of respect or love or even the air she breathed. Her imagination, her intellect, her beauty, none of her unique gifts mattered; she was forbidden to shine. And worst of all, she began to believe the lies. She believed that she was dumb, that she was ugly, that her faith made her a second-rate human being.

In her Berlin apartment building, young Susanna Sher walked down hallways plastered with anti-Semitic posters torn from the pages of *Der Stürmer*. One day she joined her father for a neighborhood stroll. Kids on the street called out, "Dirty Jews!" and spit on her father's back. He kept walking, silently, eyes straight ahead. Another day, one of her father's own employees beat him up and threatened to kill him. There was nothing her father, a proud man, could do.

In Laupheim, hometown of Carl Laemmle, the high jumper Gretel Bergmann

*Members of the Hitler Youth parade past Nazi officials in Nuremberg in 1933. German children were indoctrinated with Nazi propaganda, including vicious anti-Semitism. Fritz Sieweke, a Hitler Youth official who had attended a basketball camp in Massachusetts, helped convince German Olympic officials to add the sport to the 1936 Games.* (U.S. Holocaust Memorial Museum, courtesy of William O. McWorkman)

lived a carefree childhood before Hitler came to power. She ate plums, peaches, and apples straight from the tree; collected frogs, lizards, and salamanders; skinny-dipped under waterfalls and crawled under her covers to read books by flashlight. In the winter, she skated and skied; the best part was drinking hot chocolate afterward. She played soccer, went to synagogue on Yom Kippur and Rosh Hashanah, and by the time she was nineteen, the Nazis ruled her country and she had a boyfriend. Those last two things shouldn't be related, but in Nazi Germany the government cared who you dated. Gretel was Jewish, and Rudy wasn't. It was a forbidden love, increasingly dangerous for both of them. Gretel and Rudy felt safe meeting only under the cover of night, in the sanctuary of a friend's garden, the insane whims of a dictator tearing their hearts apart. Many years later, Bergmann recalled her last night together with Rudy.

"Once again, our friend's garden would be our refuge, only this time there would be an agonizing finality to it. And so we met. We had fallen in love less than a year ago, dreaming of a happy future, a future now confined to the agonizingly short time left of this night. The pain was almost unbearable; the agony, the depression, the despair of what was before us led down a path we had not taken before. The lifetime we had planned to be together would be over when morning came, and we devoted these few hours to expressing the deep love we had for each other. These few hours also were a symbol of our defiance of the evil Hitler stood for. It was a night when the dark seemed to rush toward the dawn with alarming speed, and when the sky began to lighten we knew that reality, no matter how hurtful, no longer could be pushed away. We held each other in an embrace that we wanted to last for eternity. We cried. We kissed. We parted. We walked off in opposite directions, not daring to look back."

Hertha Beese had lived in Berlin her entire life. When the Nazis came to power in 1933, her neighbor was forced to flee after making remarks critical of Hitler, barely escaping out a window when Nazis raided his home. Hertha rescued the baby the man left behind. Across the street, storm troopers dragged a school principal from his apartment; Hertha could hear the screams of the man's wife as he was killed, thrown down a flight of stairs. Friends went missing, presumed to be tortured in concentration camps. *Was he Jewish? Was he a Socialist?* No one knew or much cared before. Now such a label could be a death sentence.

Joachim Prinz, rabbi at Berlin's largest synagogue, had visited Al Miller's apartment many times and had performed his brother's bar mitzvah. Many of Berlin's Jewish people considered themselves more German than Jewish, but in response to Nazi persecution they began to cling closer together. As the spiritual leader of such a vulnerable group of people, Prinz later wrote that he felt an acute responsibility to preach that the "anvil was nobler than the hammer," to make Berlin's Jewish citizens feel superior, not despite but because they were targets of hate and murder. To live under a dictatorship, he understood, meant living in a constant state of fearful suspense. Hitler's dreams, or nightmares, would determine their fate from day to day.

"The press and radio depicted Jews as ugly, groveling, lecherous, power-hungry, and devious," wrote Michael Meyer in an introduction to Prinz's autobiography. "They needed to hear the opposite: that they were beautiful, noble human beings and that they had made a magnificent contribution to Western civilization. While swimming in a sea of hostile propaganda, they needed to nurture self-respect."

On April 1, 1933, the Nazis had carried out a boycott of Jewish businesses throughout Germany. Non-Jewish people who entered these stores were photographed and later beaten or arrested. Jewish people felt the suffocating power of their own countrymen turning against them. The night before the boycott was a Friday, the beginning of the Sabbath, and Prinz's synagogue was packed, buzzing with a "mixture of hope and fear, of trembling and pride." As always, two Gestapo agents sat in the front row, listening to every word, their presence meant

*On April 1, 1933, the Nazis staged a nationwide boycott of Jewish-owned businesses, part of the regime's campaign to persecute Jewish people. Here, a German civilian wearing a Nazi armband holds a sheaf of anti-Jewish signs, while Nazi storm troopers paste them on a store window.* (U.S. Holocaust Memorial Museum, courtesy of National Archives)

to intimidate. Still, Prinz felt the strength of old prayers coming to life with new shades of meaning and rebellion, and he was taken aback when it came time to sing the Shema, Judaism's most essential prayer. A cantor was prepared to sing, accompanied by a choir and organ, but was drowned out by the congregation. "All of us cried," Prinz recalled, "but, nevertheless, we sang. We sang through our tears, and although it may not have been musically perfect, the singing was like a great Jewish symphony that underscored our fate—that we were going to bear it with pride and dignity, and that come what may, we would fight for our lives." Leaving the synagogue, Prinz believed, his people felt strong and united. "There was no longer a stranger among us. We were all related, related by blood that was to be shed and by life that could be snuffed out."

Gad Beck was thirteen years old when the Olympics came to Berlin. His father was Jewish, his mom Christian. At the flag-raising ceremony each day at school, he and the other children who were considered Jewish were made to stand against a wall, apart from the other students, who stood with arms raised in the Hitler salute, singing songs and staring daggers at Gad as they raised the swastika flag. One day he won a footrace in a school competition but wasn't allowed to receive the medal. He stood against a poplar tree and sobbed; all hope had been drained from a bright and energetic boy. "I can't do it! I can't do it! What have I done to them?" he cried to his mother. He was being destroyed and he knew it.

The violence, the intimidation, the bigotry, the cruelty, the lies: this was the Germany of 1936.

This was the nation that summoned the youth of the world to compete in the Olympic Games.

And the world came marching in.

# CHAPTER SEVENTEEN

# The Grandest Show

August 1, 1936

The opening ceremonies of the eleventh Olympic Games included highly symbolic Nazi rituals: Hitler visiting Berlin's Tomb of the Unknown Soldier, a demonstration by the Hitler Youth, and the arrival of the Olympic flame from Greece, an Olympic "tradition" invented for the Nazi Olympics by Carl Diem. At the Reichssportfeld, 110,000 spectators gathered in the Olympic Stadium, and the airship *Hindenburg* buzzed slowly overhead, flying so low that people in the stadium could not only see the Olympic flag fluttering behind the ship and the swastika painted on its tailfin, but even lock eyes with passengers in the ship's cabin.

Hundreds of thousands of people lined the streets, listening to updates on loudspeakers placed overhead. The crowd was held back from the rain-slick roads by thousands of uniformed Nazis, who formed a human retaining wall, locking arms along the city's main thoroughfare in preparation for the arrival of Hitler's motorcade.

*Adolf Hitler's motorcade makes its way through Berlin's rain-slick streets and past the famed Brandenburg Gate on the way to the opening ceremonies. Thousands of onlookers crowded the roadside.* (U.S. Holocaust Memorial Museum, courtesy of National Archives)

Here was the ultimate visual expression of the Nazi state, a festival of militarism, nationalism, and totalitarian precision and symbolism. Nothing was left to chance; everything was in its place.

And then a glorious display of spontaneous humanity.

Somehow, blissfully unaware of his surroundings, a solitary man on a bicycle turned a corner and coasted onto Berlin's grand boulevard, Unter den Linden.

He pedaled along, paying no mind to the multitudes on the street, even as they cheered him along, even as the people in back lifted their homemade periscopes to get a better view. Nobody knew who this man was, why he was there, or how he'd made it past all the guards, but there he was, an unwitting symbol of freedom.

There was a playfulness and innocence to the oblivious cyclist unlike anything else in Berlin that day. As the American basketball players traveled by bus to the Olympic Stadium, Francis Johnson looked out the window, stunned by the number of soldiers on the streets. When Johnson and his teammates arrived outside the stadium, they joined athletes from other nations on the Maifeld, a grassy area lined with tall trees that had been transplanted onto the site just for the occasion. James LuValle, an African American 400-meter runner from Los Angeles, took note of the contrast. "On one side I had 55 nations who were there to see who could run the fastest, who could jump the highest, who could dive with the most beauty," he said. "On the other side, we had over 50,000 ready to go to war that day."

Meanwhile, Francis Johnson struck up a conversation with a German soldier, commenting on the dreary weather. "It never rains on Hitler," the German replied. "It will clear up."

Next thing Johnson knew, Hitler's motorcade arrived at the stadium and the clouds parted. Hitler and his entourage made their way through the middle of the field, and the American athletes, unaware or unconcerned about protocol, broke from their holding spot and rushed toward the dictator to get a closer look. Even surrounded by armed guards, Hitler appeared disturbed to see so many people coming toward him, the American javelin thrower Malcolm Metcalf recalled. "I didn't have a javelin with me," Metcalf said years later, "or I could have changed world history."

Hitler made his dramatic entry into the stadium at precisely four p.m., greeted by thunderous cheers and repeated salutes from the mostly German crowd. To some American ears, the shouts of *"Sieg Heil"* sounded like college football chants, and they may have been on to something. One of Hitler's friends, Putzi Hanfstaengl, had attended college at Harvard, where he composed songs for Crimson football games. As an early Nazi admirer, Hanfstaengl aided the cause by composing marches for the brownshirts and Hitler Youth and suggested the *Sieg Heil* (Hail Victory) chant, which he patterned after a Harvard football cheer.

*Flanked by members of the International Olympic Committee (wearing medallions around their necks), Adolf Hitler enters the Olympic Stadium for the opening ceremonies.* (U.S. Holocaust Memorial Museum, courtesy of Rosemarie Stone)

The Greek Olympic team, as was tradition, led the parade of nations into the stadium at 4:14 p.m., passing by Hitler with arms raised in salute. This became a favorite pastime of the crowd, watching to see how each nation acknowledged Hitler as they marched past his box. Countries that offered the Hitler salute, or a similar-looking "Olympic Salute," were greeted with lusty cheers. The Argentinian athletes turned their eyes toward Hitler; the Swiss flag bearer tossed his flag high into the air over and over; the Bulgarians goose-stepped around the track. Overcast skies only amplified the bright colors of all nations; the red fezzes of the Egyptians, the baby-blue jackets of the Indians, the snow-white outfits of the Icelanders.

Sylvia Weaver, a society and fashion correspondent from the *Los Angeles Times* dispatched to Berlin to report on the social scene, sat in awe in the press box, surrounded by blue hydrangeas, marveling at the spectacle taking shape before her eyes. "Zeus, in his golden days," she gushed, "never witnessed a show as grand as this one." She was impressed by the colors of unbridled power and aristocracy, noting how the "handsome blue, green and black uniforms of the German army, the [Führer's] private bodyguard and the air force mingle with the brown of the storm troops and the gold of the Olympic chains worn by the International Olympic Committee." Weaver's *Times* colleague Bill Henry recalled that just three years earlier, the Nazis had recoiled at the very idea of the Olympics, dismissing them as a Jewish international enterprise. But now, he said, the "showmen of the Third Reich" had seized upon the propaganda value of the event's pageantry. "Staging of the Olympics in the past has been in the hands of amateurs," he wrote. "Here, the work has been done by professionals, and by the most talented, resourceful and successful professionals in history."

In convincing Hitler that the Olympics would generate enormous international propaganda opportunities, Goebbels had articulated a belief that was at the core of his entire philosophy of public persuasion. "Think of the press," he said, "as a great keyboard on which the government can play." The writers from Los Angeles, at least, were willing to be played.

Before the people of LA could read the words of Henry and Weaver in the next day's paper, however, they gathered around their radios, tuned to KECA and KHJ, and listened live to the ceremonies, hearing a mix of whistles and cheers when American gymnast Al Jochim led the U.S. delegation into the stadium just behind the team from Uruguay. Bill Wheatley, the Refiners basketball player from Gypsum, Kansas, felt his entire body tingling with goose bumps when he emerged from the tunnel into the pulsating arena. Marty Glickman, a Jewish sprinter from New York, looked over at Hitler as he approached his box. Glickman smiled; with his tiny mustache, Hitler reminded him of the comic silent film actor Charlie Chaplin. Big Joe Fortenberry was amused, too. Observing the German crowd's hysteria, the way people reacted wildly to their Führer's every move, he couldn't help but laugh. Hitler would have been no match on the bare-knuckle boxing circuit of West Texas. "How could a little guy like that have so much control over these people?" he recalled. "It was a comedy to us Americans. They treated him like he was their God."

Many Germans didn't find it funny, however, when the Americans walked casually past Hitler's box. In keeping with American custom, Jochim, a Berlin-born immigrant, didn't dip the American flag in deference as other countries' flag bearers had done. The athletes behind him didn't give a Hitler salute, but instead placed their right hands over their hearts. From pockets of the stadium came a symphony of whistles, the European equivalent of boos. Francis Johnson's wife, Lucille, rose from her seat in the stadium to watch her husband and his basketball teammates march by. The boys were assigned to group seven of the eight American marching contingents, striding side by side with members of the soccer and field hockey teams, a lowly position ahead of only the canoeing, field handball, and baseball squads. As she stood and cheered with pride, Lucille Johnson felt a shooting pain in her back. A German man had punched her, enraged that her husband and the other Americans had disrespected Hitler.

A day that began with a sweet and symbolic imperfection, the oblivious cyclist, ended with a flourish of spontaneous rebellion, too.

As the opening ceremonies came to a close, hundreds of birds were released from cardboard cages placed throughout the stadium. Some thought these were doves, the traditional symbol of peace, but in fact they were carrier pigeons supplied by the German military. As the pigeons soared into the sky, they flitted back and forth above the stadium's infield, where the athletes of the world stood at attention. Cannons were fired, unintentionally startling the birds.

Several American athletes then felt drops of white liquid land on their blue jackets.

As a swarm of pigeons pooped on them, the Americans looked up at a dictator who reminded them of a slapstick comedian and laughed at the absurdity of it all.

# CHAPTER EIGHTEEN

# Village People

An apple is an apple and a steak is a steak, but not much else in the Olympic Village was exactly what it appeared to be.

The enchanted forest of birch trees surrounding the athletes' lodges, with its gently sloping hills and meandering paths, its ducks, deer, and rabbits, had all been created from scratch—like a movie set at Carl Laemmle's Universal City—in the months leading up to the Games. Even the squirrels were trucked in.

The helpful women at the information desk in the main lodge? They were undercover police officers, trained to intercept and inspect the athletes' incoming mail. On August 7, the day the Olympic basketball tournament began, these spies confiscated seventy-four anti-Nazi letters disguised as good-luck messages to British Olympians.

*Here's the Olympic Village the Germans built for male athletes competing in the '36 Games. The circular building to the left is the dining hall. The long, rectangular buildings where the athletes slept were each named after towns in Germany. The American basketball team stayed in the Dessau cabin.* (McPherson Museum)

The men in plain clothes hastily leaving the Village just as the first athletes arrived? Not civilians, but members of the German military's Condor Legion, completing a training regimen and on their way to conduct bombing raids for the fascist Nationalists in the Spanish Civil War.

The placid lake next to the sauna built for the Finns? The site of underwater training exercises for German soldiers.

Even the boys assigned as guides for each team were members of the Hitler Youth, ordered not just to provide directions and accompany athletes into town but to keep tabs on the visitors and steer them away from sites the Nazis would rather they not see.

If the trappings surrounding the 1936 Olympics were one gigantic exercise in subterfuge, a bright shining lie, it was in the Olympic Village where the deception was most orchestrated and, in many cases, the most transparent.

Even so, any athlete who lived there in the summer of 1936 would tell you it was one heck of a fun place to be.

The Village was where many Olympians first witnessed the new invention television. The Germans had placed small black-and-white sets in communal areas, broadcasting blurry images of live sports for the first time in history.

Each night after dinner, athletes gathered in a one-thousand-seat theater to watch newsreel highlights from the previous day's competition and to enjoy live performances from the world's finest entertainers. On some nights, the festivities concluded with fireworks, on others with outdoor concerts illuminated by torchlight.

After the entertainers took their last bows, many athletes ventured into the surrounding woods, where the Village's strict "no women allowed" rule was violated nightly. German authorities brought in prostitutes to socialize with white—and only white—athletes. Other Olympians retired to their barracks for late-night card games. Sam Balter and his wife, Mildred, had split their entire $35 savings before he left for Europe. He fattened his thin wallet with blackjack winnings. Willard Schmidt found guys who knew how to play bridge.

If the SS *Manhattan* had served as a floating buffet table, the food service in the Village was even more remarkable. Hundreds of German chefs spent months learning to cook every type of world cuisine; each nation had its own dining room, kitchen staff, and menu. Steaks cooked pink in the center for the Chileans. Six oranges a day for the Brazilians. Pasta for the Italians. Vegetarian options for the

Indians. Ice cream and sixteen varieties of chewing gum for the Americans. By the Games' end, the athletes of the world had consumed 91 pigs, 646 sheep and lambs, 1,800 pounds of mushrooms, 8,400 pounds of jams and jellies, 19,000 gallons of milk, 232,000 eggs, and 81 sacks of coffee.

The Australians may have brought their own kangaroo to the Village, but virtually everything else imaginable was provided by the Germans, even a dentist's office where sprinter Archie Williams had a tooth filled. One day, Schmidt went in for a haircut at the Village barbershop and was startled by a commotion outside. The professional German heavyweight boxer and international celebrity Max Schmeling was visiting the Village. Athletes from around the world surrounded him, posing for photographs and collecting autographs. But Schmeling wasn't the only notable German visitor.

One day Herb Wildman, the water polo goalkeeper, decided to go for a swim. Walking through the Village wearing only his swim trunks and a towel draped over his shoulder, he froze in his tracks when a squad of four large black cars approached him. The first car came skidding to a halt, and a portly military official stepped out. Armed SS officers jumped out of the other three vehicles, striking a threatening pose. Wildman thought that was funny—as if he could have hidden a weapon in his swimming suit. The fat man introduced himself: he was Hermann Göring, Hitler's right-hand man, one of the creators of the Gestapo (the Nazis' brutal secret police force) and commander of the Luftwaffe, the German air force. Following World War II, Göring would be tried, convicted, and sentenced to death for crimes against humanity. But on this day, he played the role of friendly host, engaging in conversation with Wildman for nearly twenty minutes. *How are the facilities? How are you being treated? How's the food? What are your impressions of Germany?* "He was so courteous that I couldn't believe, even after this thing was over, the stories we heard about him," Wildman recalled decades later. "He was so gracious a man."

*Members of the U.S. Olympic basketball team relax outside their cabin in the Olympic Village. One day, German dictator Adolf Hitler and his girlfriend, Eva Braun, surprised the players by appearing here and asking a few questions about their experience in Berlin.* (McPherson Museum)

One day at the Dessau lodge, home of the American basketball team, Francis Johnson, Bill Wheatley, and other players were relaxing on lounge chairs when a recognizable figure appeared before them. It was Adolf Hitler with his girlfriend, Eva Braun. The basketball players were shocked to see the couple standing on their patio. The dictator engaged in small talk with the Americans for a few minutes, then snapped up his right arm in the familiar Nazi salute and was gone.

While the male athletes luxuriated in the pleasures of a man-made paradise, the world's best female athletes experienced far less than equal treatment. There was no Olympic Village for women, just a dormitory, the Friesenhaus, adjacent to

*American basketball player Tex Gibbons stands outside the Dessau cabin at the Olympic Village wearing his official USA sweat suit. Gibbons had injured his arm in an auto accident just before boarding the ship to Germany.* (McPherson Museum)

the Reichssportfeld. Some women considered the location an advantage; they lived much closer to the site of the athletic competitions than the men. But that was the only silver lining. Single beds with mattresses stuffed with straw. Bathrooms and showers way down at the end of the hall. A cranky old baroness watching over the place. No special chefs, no heaping piles of fruit. Iris Cummings, an American swimmer, yearned for a single orange. She never got one. Instead: Boiled cabbage. Potatoes. Boiled beef. Turnips. And that was if she happened to find a good seat at mealtime. Female athletes were served family style, sitting on both sides of long tables. As the food was passed down in large bowls, athletes at the front took however much they wanted while women at the end fought for scraps. There were no second helpings. On the night before a particular athlete's competition, there was a rare reward, a sizzling steak delivered on a platter.

The women had teenage German girls assigned as guides, and many of the American athletes later recalled one of their favorite pastimes was trying to ditch the girls on their visits to the shops and restaurants of Berlin. Hurdler Anne O'Brien recalled the best strategy. Standing in a group, some of the American women would bolt down the sidewalk in one direction, the rest in the other. Still, one sixteen-year-old German girl proved especially difficult to shake loose. She had previously lived in the U.S.; her father had been called back to a post in the German government. The girl spoke perfect English and desperately wanted to return to America.

As the American women worked hard to lose their German chaperones, the men looked for entertainment wherever they could find it. Art Mollner worked at a post office in Los Angeles when he wasn't busy practicing for the Universals. Many of his friends were avid stamp collectors, and he came to Berlin with more than $500 and orders to purchase as many Olympic stamps as possible. Mollner completed that shopping expedition in two hours and then discovered more exciting diversions. One night, he and teammate Carl Shy went out to a Berlin beer garden, where they were impressed with how much fun the German patrons were having, everyone holding steins of beer and singing along with the musicians on stage. Another time Mollner and Shy decided to ride the Berlin subway as far as they could, getting off at a stop in the country at the end of the line. Standing outside in their USA sweaters with no idea where they were, they were approached by a pair of Germans riding a motorcycle—one on the bike and one in a sidecar. The Germans invited the Americans to lunch. But with only two seats available, it took three back-and-forth trips to get everyone to the riverside restaurant. Mollner asked if Hitler wanted war. Every morning, the basketball players had marveled at the Luftwaffe planes flying over the Village. They had seen German soldiers performing war maneuvers out in the open fields of Berlin, crawling with packs on their backs and rifles in their arms. It seemed obvious. But the Germans didn't see it that way. *No, no, Hitler doesn't want war. He wants to build Germany up. He just wants to get back the land we lost in the Great War.*

But even in this capital of a dictatorship so clearly preparing for battle, the Americans discovered plenty of fun and hospitality. Frank Graham of the water polo team recalled being driven by the chauffeur of a high-ranking German military official to a nightclub playing American music. In one room, a large bologna was placed atop a greased pole; if you could climb all the way to the top, you won the sausage. The crowd erupted in huge cheers whenever anyone was successful. The Americans couldn't pull off the feat, but consolation came for Graham and his teammate Dutch McCallister when they met a pair of German sisters who took them out to see the sights of Berlin.

African American athletes found Berlin far more welcoming than most American cities. A German colonel invited James LuValle to eat dinner at his home with his wife and two daughters. "It was very pleasant," LuValle recalled. "Things like that were happening all the time. We didn't see any intolerance."

But it was there.

Carl Shy saw it when he looked through a crack in a Berlin wall at a propaganda poster depicting a Jewish man with a grotesquely huge nose.

Sam Balter saw it in the newspapers on Berlin's newsstands, with their stereotypical caricatures of Jewish people and headlines blaming them for the world's problems.

Irving "Toots" Meretsky, a Jewish member of the Canadian basketball team, saw it when he ventured into a Jewish-owned camera shop. The shelves were nearly bare, the store owners downcast. "You could tell they were scared," he recalled. "The people running the store said they didn't know what would happen to them."

Simone Schaller, a Catholic American hurdler, saw it when she went to Mass one morning and saw members of the Gestapo seated in the pews, there not for inspiration but to intimidate the priest.

Joanna de Tuscan saw it. Voted "Most Beautiful" American Olympian, the American fencer caught the eye of Hitler and was invited to attend several parties and even a political rally where she was the only American, surrounded by thousands of "middle of the road people, mamas and papas." A meeting hall bubbling with steady conversation boiled over when Hitler began to speak, his voice growing louder and louder and more animated. The mood had changed in a way that de Tuscan found alarming. "It was a total insane asylum," she recalled. "Everyone was on their feet but me. Everyone was screaming. They were standing up, they were shaking their fists. I think it was just pure hypnosis."

Iris Cummings saw it when she counted the soldiers goose-stepping past her each day and listened to how the girl guides spoke with such nationalistic fervor: *We are trained! We are ready! We are dominant!*

Frank Graham saw it when he was invited to dinner at the home of an average German family. Though his hosts spoke little English and Graham spoke little German, the message from the German father was clear. "He thought Hitler was the greatest," Graham recalled, "and the Germans were going to rule the world. He made no bones about it."

And Herb Wildman saw it. The Nazis had gone to great lengths to prevent international visitors from encountering Jewish Germans. Jewish people were denied licenses to sell soft drinks and souvenirs near the Olympic Stadium. Any foreigner interested in speaking to a Jewish person was ordered to contact the Gestapo first. The secret police raided churches and synagogues, seizing type-writers and duplicating machines so opponents of the regime couldn't prepare anti-Nazi flyers. The Nazis went so far as to give party members undercover jobs as janitors and waiters in areas where foreigners gathered, ordered to engage in small talk and influence the foreigners' opinions of Jewish people. But one day, Wildman walked down Unter den Linden admiring the shops. A young German man spotted Wildman's USA sweatshirt and invited him to sit down for a cup of tea. Wildman obliged; the man began peppering him with questions about life in the United States. Impressed by the man's curiosity, Wildman invited him to the Olympic Village to meet more American athletes.

"No, I can't come out there," the German replied.

"Oh, you don't have time?" Wildman replied.

"No, I can't come out." The German sighed.

The Olympics were a celebration of movement, a testament to precise measurement. The 100-meter dash. The 4x400-meter relay. 1,500-meter run. 26.2 miles in the marathon. But for this young man, a Jewish student at the University of Berlin, the distance that determined his fate in life was one half of a mile. Venture any farther than that from the college campus, the Gestapo warned him, and he'd be hauled off to a concentration camp.

# CHAPTER NINETEEN

# Witnesses to History

The American basketball players stared at the SS officers on the other side of the street, tall German men dressed all in black who stared back.

It was the first week of Olympic competition, and the day's track and field events were about to get under way. More than one hundred thousand spectators had rushed through eighty turnstiles into the Olympic Stadium, and the soldiers and basketball players outside could hear the buzz of the crowd. The center of attention had yet to arrive; the Americans knew where Adolf Hitler would enter the stadium and wanted to catch a glimpse. So there they stood, just off to the side of a short road that led to the private entrance for Hitler and his entourage.

The SS men were all at least six two or six three, and they made for an imposing sight in their crisp black uniforms, even more so when they snapped to attention

*American basketball player Bill Wheatley poses with members of Adolf Hitler's personal bodyguard unit outside the Olympic Stadium. At this point, Wheatley and his teammates considered the Nazis more of a curiosity than a threat to world peace. Just over five years later, Americans and Nazis would be mortal enemies in World War II.* (McPherson Museum)

upon the arrival of Hitler's motorcade. When the dictator stepped out of his car, the guards stretched their right arms in salute; Hitler returned the gesture and walked into the stadium with Hermann Göring by his side.

Joe Fortenberry, Francis Johnson, Bill Wheatley, and the rest of the boys scrambled into the stadium as fast as they could. They made it inside before Hitler entered his private box. When he did, it seemed that 110,000 people jumped to their feet in unison, thrusting out their arms, yelling, *"Heil Hitler,"* at the top of their lungs and sending a tremble through the limestone walls of the enormous stadium.

The basketball players made their way onto the infield inside the oval track, where they could get a close-up view of the action. There they stood on the grandest sporting stage the modern world had ever seen. A bell tower at one end of the arena stood 247 feet high; a scoreboard at the other was large enough for nine lines of text with up to sixty-three characters each. The world's media gathered in a 193-foot-long press box, complete with forty-six writing desks and twenty radio transmitters. The *Hindenburg* floated above the scene, and Nazi-commissioned documentary filmmaker Leni Riefenstahl, a former actress in a Universal Pictures movie produced by Carl Laemmle, instructed her crew of camera operators on

*Bill Wheatley jokes around outside the Olympic Stadium wearing a German military helmet as Nazi guards lounge on the grass beside him. Note Wheatley's inscription: "Almost created a Revolution over this one." Apparently the Nazis weren't too pleased with his antics.* (McPherson Museum)

the day's assignments. They'd collect footage of the athletes, but also keep cameras trained on Hitler's every move.

The notion that Adolf Hitler presided over an Olympic Games was absurd on many levels, including one of the most basic: he was a terrible athlete. He couldn't swim or ride a horse and didn't like to exercise, lest he appear weak and shatter his image as the ruler of a "master race." He was no fan of team sports and had opposed the idea of friendly international competition until Goebbels and Diem convinced him of the propaganda value of hosting the Olympics. But once the Games began, Hitler became mesmerized by the drama of the contests, a fixture in his box at the Olympic Stadium. American journalists and athletes couldn't take their eyes off him, noting how he nervously watched the events, crossing and uncrossing his legs, fiddling with his mustache, drumming his fingers on his knees. His mood swung like a pendulum. When German athletes lost, Hitler's expression and posture betrayed his displeasure, but when they won, he leaped from his seat and beamed like a child on Christmas morning.

The German crowd's fixation on, and celebration of, victory struck foreign visitors as excessive, their choreographed expressions of nationalism not just inappropriate for an international festival of peace and brotherhood, but evidence of the mind control of the Nazi state. "Bands play German national hymns and a hundred thousand zealots . . . stretch out their arms and sing," reported Matthew Halton of the *Toronto Star*. "Something like religious ecstasy, rather than . . . sporting enthusiasm, is the spirit abroad here today."

Nazis in black boots and others in plain clothes kept a close eye on German

*Under the threatening and watchful eye of German soldiers, German fans at the opening ceremonies behaved as one, saluting dictator Adolf Hitler. Their chants of "Sieg Heil" were patterned after a Harvard football cheer.*
(U.S. Holocaust Memorial Museum, courtesy of National Archives)

spectators, enforcing displays of patriotism—once and forever a sure sign of political weakness. Anyone who didn't stand, salute, and join in the chants was followed and arrested when they left the stadium.

American swimmer Iris Cummings attended the track competition with her mom and the mother of teammate Marjorie Gestring, who had German relatives. Mrs. Gestring brought a German friend with her, a woman who opposed the Nazis. When the crowd stood to salute Hitler, the woman squeezed between Cummings's mother and Gestring, arms tight to her sides, hiding her small, brave act of resistance from the gaze of black-booted soldiers behind her.

American journalist Fred Farrell recognized the danger inherent in this toxic mix of nationalism and militarism, essentially predicting World War II. "I have an idea these Olympic Games will have repercussions that will not help toward the amity of nations as they are supposed to. There will be dark trouble clouds along the horizon. They may develop into thunderstorms." Polish diplomat Józef Lipski shared a similar concern: people who could be so well choreographed for a sporting event could also be mobilized just as smoothly for war.

The war these men anticipated was three years away, officially beginning when Hitler invaded Poland in 1939. But more immediate horrors awaited Germany's Jewish people. While the sixteen days of the Olympic Games provided a temporary respite from the most egregious acts of anti-Semitism, it was no secret that the Nazis were preparing to unleash a new round of terror once the Games were over. Goebbels had said as much, publicly encouraging Nazi party affiliates to save their energy until after the Games. "When the Olympics are over," Nazi storm troopers had sung as they marched through the city's streets, "we'll beat the Jews to a pulp."

Al Miller, the thirteen-year-old Jewish boy from Berlin, would flee Germany by himself less than a year later, his parents a year after that. His uncle would remain, only to be murdered in the Auschwitz concentration camp.

But all that was in the future. For now, Miller was a wide-eyed kid, a sports fan thrilled to witness the Olympics in his hometown. And he had a ticket.

Al didn't have an assigned seat, just "standing room only." That wasn't ideal for a thirteen-year-old stuck behind a wall of adults craning their necks to see the action, so he twisted and contorted his body to the front of the pack. Just as he squeezed through, Hitler entered his box. Miller could see the man who hated him, but what struck Miller was what he heard: a jubilant crowd shouting, *"Heil Hitler,"* over and over, louder and louder, and when the shouting died down it would pick back up again, seemingly with no end.

*German fans displayed a throaty nationalism that was unsettling to many visitors who viewed the Olympics as an international gathering of peace and goodwill.* (U.S. Holocaust Memorial Museum, courtesy of National Archives)

Then there was shouting of another sort, fans gasping at the incredible performance of an American on the track. Down at field level, Art Mollner admired the graceful stride of the man leading the pack of runners: he looked as relaxed as a man in a rocking chair. In his private box adjacent to Nazi leaders and dignitaries,

American novelist Thomas Wolfe jumped out of his seat, screaming with joy. Hitler leaned over to see who was making all the commotion, glaring at the American. The crowd then quieted as the public-address commentator came on the loudspeaker, announcing a gold medal for the United States by the undisputed star of these Games, the great African American sprinter Jesse Owens.

Owens's spectacular performance in Berlin remains etched in the world's collective memory. But for Al Miller, the scene was memorable for another reason, one he would vividly recall more than eighty years later.

Jesse Owens, the fastest man on earth, was the first black man he'd ever seen.

# CHAPTER TWENTY

# Neutral Zone

I n the decades to come, Jesse Owens's record-setting performance in Berlin, the gold medals he won in the 100, 200, long jump, and 4x100 relay, would be celebrated as a powerful rebuke of Hitler. A black man's incredible success in a crucible of hate served as the ultimate rejection of the idea of white supremacy. But this conventional wisdom is an oversimplification on two levels.

First, Owens wasn't the only African American star in Berlin, even in his own events. In the 100, black teammate Ralph Metcalfe finished just one-tenth of a second behind him to win the silver medal. In the 200, black teammate Mack Robinson won the silver, four-tenths of a second behind Owens. Metcalfe joined Owens on the 4x100 relay team. In all, the eighteen African American members of the U.S. team earned fourteen medals in Berlin, eight of them gold, one-fourth of

*American sprinter Jesse Owens proudly displays three of the four gold medals he won in Berlin. He's wearing a wreath that was presented to medalists. An oak sapling, also presented to medalists, rests on the table. Owens, a star of the Games, was disparaged by both racist Germans and Americans.* (U.S. Holocaust Memorial Museum, courtesy of National Archives)

the U.S. medal count. The entire African American contingent, not just Owens, took the world by storm. Perpetuating the idea that Owens alone shined not only robs others of their due but leaves the impression that African American greatness at the '36 Games was an exception rather than the rule.

Second, the performance of these black athletes didn't disprove white supremacy, at least among those who believed in it, in either Germany or the United States. In the minds of legions of detractors, there was no way for black people to win; the truth didn't matter. Stereotypes and hate were so deeply ingrained that any fact or fiction could be used to confirm them. If black people performed poorly, that "proved" white people were superior. If black people were victorious, that "proved" they had unfair advantages as a subhuman race. When black Americans emerged as the stars of the Berlin Olympics' first days of track competition, Joseph Goebbels wrote in his diary that "white humanity should be ashamed of itself." He meant not only for losing, but for even allowing black people to compete. When Baldur von Schirach, leader of the Hitler Youth, suggested to Adolf Hitler that posing for a photo with the champion Owens would be good publicity, Hitler was repulsed by the idea. "The Americans ought to be ashamed of themselves for letting their medals be won by Negroes," he replied in anger. "I myself would never shake hands with one of them."

American assistant track coach Dean Cromwell revealed the mind-set that led white people to dismiss the athletic feats of black people. In their bigoted minds, black people were near-animals, giving them an unfair athletic advantage over more "refined" white competitors. "It was not that long ago," Cromwell said of the

**LEHMAN ACTS IN REFORMATORY BIAS**

# NEW YORK
# Amsterdam News

*HARLEM'S LARGEST WEEKLY NEWSPAPER*

**COMPLETE**

Issued and published every Saturday by Powell-Savory Corp.
Entered as second-class matter, Post Office, New York, N.Y.

NEW YORK, SATURDAY, AUGUST 8, 1936    5 CENTS In Metropolitan Area Elsewhere 10 Cents    VOL. XXVII. NO. 35

# NEGRO HEROES PILE UP
# 70 OF 187 U. S. POINTS

## HEAD OF STATE TOLD ILLS AT GIRLS' SCHOOL

**Says Discrimination Is "Indefensible" at a Public Institution**

(Special to The Amsterdam News)

ALBANY, Aug. 6.—Calling racial discrimination in a state institution "indefensible," Governor Herbert H. Lehman today (Thursday) addressed an unequivocal letter to Victor F. Ridder, chairman of the State Board of Social Welfare, calling his attention to charges of discrimination against Negro girls in the state supporting training school-reformatory at Hudson.

The governor's action came seventeen hours after a committee of New Yorkers had met with the state's executive and members of his staff in a conference lasting one hour and thirty minutes.

"All groups in the school," wrote the governor, "must, of course, be placed on absolute equality with regard to living accommodations and other facilities. There should be no separation in the institution along racial-lines."

Headed by Dr. Marshall Ross, surgeon, left to West 129th street, the committee came to Albany at the invitation of the Governor, who had received complaints from citizens in

## *Negro to Get Square Deal From Somervell*

**New WPA Chief, a West Pointer, Promises There Will Be No Cause to Complain, but Begs Time to Get Acquainted**

"If Negroes were satisfied with the way things went under Commissioner Ridder, they will have no cause to complain now. I shall do everything in my power to see that they get a square deal," Lieut.-Col. Brehon Burke Somervell told an Amsterdam News representative Wednesday at the new WPA headquarters at 70 Columbus avenue.

Succeeding Victor F. Ridder, whose resignation became effective last Saturday, as Works Progress Administrator for New York City, Col. Somervell has had much engineering experience here and in Europe. Its came here directly from Florida, where he was engineer in charge of the Atlantic-Gulf ship canal project.

The new administrator said that, although he knew little about the charges of discrimination in the local setup, he should be able to cope with any situation that might arise, since he had had much experience with Negroes in the South.

**Questioned on Attitude**

"What is your attitude about attempts to discriminate against Negroes in the WPA setup in New York City?" Col. Somervell was asked.

"I know of no cases of discrimination," he answered. "Of course, I have only been here two days... But through our Negro relations committee, headed by Mr. Foster, we will take care of any such case that comes to our attention."

Col. Somervell referred to Lemuel

## BOY HELD FOR KILLING AFTER RACIAL 'WAR'

**Protests Innocence in Brooklyn Outbreak —Seize Juveniles**

Protesting his innocence, Smith Brown, 18, was being held yesterday for a hearing Tuesday on a charge of slaying Mario Vella in a Brooklyn gang war of colored and white youths.

Brown, who lives at 47 Clifton place, Brooklyn, was arrested Tuesday following a clash Monday night in the Port Greene section. He admitted that he had taken part in a previous clash of the races, but said he was not present when Vella was struck so hard with a broomstick that he died of a fractured skull.

Clashes broke out last Friday, when a group of white boys and defeated in a pitched battle and proposed a return fracas.

After the fatal encounter, in which the whites were again dispersed, police took into custody Clinton Collins, 13; John White, 15, of 51 and 53 Clifton place, respectively; Paul Fulton, 15, 233 Greene avenue, and Charles Riley, 378 Grand avenue

They were held in bail of $500 each for hearings Tuesday on charges of juvenile delinquency. Justice Hannon urged that they remain in custody to prevent any new outbreaks.

## OWENS CAPTURES 3 CROWNS AT BERLIN; 2 OTHERS IN FIRST

**Buckeye Bullet Chalks Up 3 World Records Before 100,000—Johnson Smashes Mark for Jump as Woodruff Takes 800**

**NEGROES SCORE THREE SMALL-SLAMS**

**Phil Edwards Third in 800 and Fifth in 1,500—Metcalfe Follows Ohioan in 100 —Robinson Second Man in 200**

**By WILLIAM C. CHASE,**
*Amsterdam News Staff Correspondent*

BERLIN, Aug. 6.—When the good ship Manhattan left its berth with the United States Olympic team for its foreign invasion, the experts claimed that it bore the strongest track and field teams to have ever left the American shores. Ten Negro boys were on that boat as track and field Olympic entries, and these ten boys, so the critics said, were the strongest part of the American forces in that division. They figured that these dusky athletes would gather in some six first places, five second places

*An African American newspaper in New York proudly hailed the achievements of black athletes in Berlin. Many white sportswriters, however, referred to the black American superstars in racist terms and belittled their achievements.*
(U.S. Holocaust Memorial Museum, courtesy of Library of Congress)

black athlete, "that his ability to spring and jump was a life-and-death matter to him in the jungle."

Louis Lyons, a columnist from the *Boston Globe*, was one of the few white American journalists to challenge the slurs spewed by observers from both sides of the Atlantic, responding with actual facts. "The best the Nazis have been able to do with the racial problem created by Jesse Owens & Co is to theorize that these represent a race of American helots, more nearly akin to the panther and the jack rabbit than to their Aryan competitors," he wrote. "This is a view that conveniently disregards the fact that one of these colored athletes is a Phi Beta Kappa scholarship man, one is in medical school, one a law student and the others are meeting the requirements of American college life."

The bigoted comments, along with the fact that the world's grandest sporting event was allowed to be hosted by the Nazis in the first place, illustrate an uncomfortable truth for advocates of sports. To this day, many people believe without question the philosophy popularized by men such as Luther Gulick, James Naismith, and Avery Brundage: that sports are inherently good. Organized athletics cultivate positive attributes, they believe, including self-discipline, work ethic ,and sportsmanship. Qualities such as fairness, respect, and morality are inherent in athletics, goes the reasoning, and nowhere in life is the playing field as level for all participants as it is in the world of sports, where success and failure are determined, without favor, by one's performance. By appreciating the achievements of athletes from all ethnicities, religions, genders, and nations, these people further believe, we are brought closer together as one human race. There is appeal in the notion that even in a war-torn and hate-filled world, young people from all nations can come together to live and compete in peace.

There were some examples of this in Berlin. By all accounts, the athletes of the world got along well at the Olympic Village, and Jesse Owens struck up a close friendship with Luz Long, his German rival in the long jump, that lasted until Long was killed in World War II. None of this would have happened had there been an American boycott. As author Jeremy Schaap writes in *Triumph*, his book on Owens, "if not for [Avery] Brundage's pigheadedness, cunning, Germanophilia, anti-Semitism, and deep-rooted bigotry, Jesse Owens would never have become an Olympian," let alone a legendary figure.

Even so, rather than studying the Games of '36 as an example only of the positive value of sports, perhaps we should more closely examine them as a case study of the limitations of sports. Consider all that unfolded in Berlin for the American team. When it came time for the men's 4x100 relay, two runners slated to be on the team, Marty Glickman and Sam Stoller, were dropped at the last minute without rational explanation. It was Stoller's twenty-first birthday; he spent the occasion not celebrating a gold medal victory but sobbing in his bed at the Olympic Village. Why were Glickman and Stoller, two of the rare American athletes in history to arrive at the Games and never have a chance to compete, benched? They were the only Jewish members of the U.S. track team. Many people believe American coaches and officials acted to spare Hitler the "embarrassment" of two Jewish athletes winning gold. Others say favoritism, not anti-Semitism, was at play. Dropping the pair allowed two sprinters from Dean Cromwell's team at the University of Southern California to compete. Either way, sports had provided a venue for a breach in ethics and fairness.

On the women's team, a similar scenario played out when Louise Stokes was told she wouldn't compete in the 4x100 relay. For the African American Stokes, it was the second time she was denied the opportunity she had worked hard to earn. At the 1932 Olympics in Los Angeles, she had also been pulled from the race. Two times she had been on the verge of becoming the first African American woman to compete in the Olympics, and twice she was denied. Even on the way to the '32 Games she had been victimized. White teammate Babe Didrikson, often lauded as the first superstar American female athlete and therefore a champion for women's rights, poured a pitcher of cold water on Stokes and black teammate Tidye Pickett on the train to LA.

"Sport as an ideal is not a force for positive social good," says Sara Bloomfield, director of the U.S. Holocaust Museum. "Sport is a neutral form. It needs positive underpinnings. And, it requires human beings [running it] to assume a sense of responsibility."

There was no starker example of the neutrality of sport than the stories of the men who medaled in Berlin's 200-meter sprint. All three men competed in the same event on the same track on August 5, 1936, finishing within 0.6 seconds of each other. Yet their trajectories could not be more different. Sport proved only to be a neutral platform from which their lives evolved.

Atop the victory stand was champion Jesse Owens, forever to be regarded as a symbol of the triumph of good over evil and an example of the democracy of sport: give an athlete a fair shot and his or her talent can't be denied, even in the most hostile circumstances.

Next to Owens, a silver medal draped the neck of Mack Robinson, his African American teammate. Four-tenths of a second too slow, he lived out the rest of his life in obscurity. But you have heard of Robinson's younger brother. To this day, he's recognized as the most important sports pioneer of all time. His name was Jackie, and he played a little baseball.

And what became of the third-place finisher, Tinus Osendarp of Holland, hailed by the sports media of 1936 as the "fastest white man in the world"? While in Berlin for the Olympics, Osendarp began to admire the Nazis. When Hitler's army invaded his homeland in 1940, he gladly joined the Nazi secret police.

Osendarp chased down Jewish people and freedom fighters and sent them to die in prison.

# CHAPTER TWENTY-ONE

# 110,000 Bored Germans

With four-inch-wide white tape pressed down on the grass of the Olympic Stadium serving as foul lines and a soccer goal used as a backstop behind home plate, two teams of obscure American amateur baseball players drawn from college and club teams played a seven-inning exhibition game on August 12, 1936, invited by German Olympic officials to demonstrate their sport. Turns out basketball wasn't the only American pastime introduced to the Germans in Berlin in the summer of '36.

At a time when the mighty New York Yankees led Major League Baseball with an average attendance of 12,687, this meaningless game drew nearly ten times as many fans, 110,000, the most ever to watch a baseball game at that point in history.

That was an amazing feat considering baseball wasn't played in Germany and

*An aerial view of the Olympic sports venues. The opening and closing ceremonies and track events took place in the 110,000-seat Olympic Stadium. The basketball games were held outdoors on converted tennis courts.* (McPherson Museum)

just about the only people who had any idea what was happening were the players and the American sportswriters in the press box.

Before the game, the German crowd cheered heartily when the Americans lined up on the basepaths and greeted the fans with a Hitler salute, an awkward moment for Herman Goldberg of Brooklyn, a catcher and the only Jewish member of either baseball team. It was just one of many such moments for Goldberg. He cringed at the sight of a magazine left in his dormitory featuring photos of Hitler and Goebbels. And one day he and Marty Glickman had been hitchhiking to Berlin when they were picked up by a pair of German soldiers. Halfway through the trip, one of the Germans asked Glickman and Goldberg to produce their passports; they had heard Goldberg slip up and use a Yiddish word when trying to communicate in broken German. As the soldiers examined the Americans' documents on the side of the highway, Goldberg listened nervously as the Nazis discussed the fact that the two U.S. athletes were Jewish. But then relief. The soldiers asked for autographs.

And now here was Goldberg, crouching behind the plate for the biggest baseball spectacle the world had ever seen, under the lights of the Olympic Stadium. That was noteworthy for two reasons. First, night games were a rarity in the U.S., with the Cincinnati Reds having played the first major-league night game just a year earlier. Second, the lights themselves weren't positioned properly for a baseball game, illuminating the action to a height of just fifty feet. Fly balls disappeared into the darkness.

As far as the German fans were concerned, the baseballs and the game itself might as well have vanished into the night and never come back. The spectators were, in the words of one American sportswriter, "unbearably bored" by the game. Thousands of fans hadn't realized the game had started and thought the players were still warming up. There were more cheers for pop-ups than base hits. Fans debated whether the catcher was "neutral" or playing for one team or the other. They laughed at the way the umpire loudly called out balls and strikes.

But with no understanding of the rules of the game, even that measure of fun lasted only so long.

Thousands of fans started heading for the exits in the third inning. By the fourth, it became a stampede; only a few thousand stragglers remained. "And thus a contest that drew the largest crowd in history," lamented the *New York Herald*

*Tribune*, "was played out to the most colossal indifference any baseball game has ever known."

Finally, the spectators let out a wild cheer. Nothing had happened in the game and the American ballplayers didn't know why.

The public-address announcer had declared, in German, that the game was almost over.

# CHAPTER TWENTY-TWO

# Tournament Time

O f the millions of people walking Berlin's crowded and colorful streets in August of 1936, only one had invented an Olympic sport, and that gave James Naismith, a humble man, a certain amount of pride.

Teams from twenty-one nations had arrived in Germany to play a game that would not have existed if not for Naismith's ingenuity.

In tribute, North American basketball fans had chipped in enough money—a collection of pennies and nickels—to send Naismith to Berlin, a well-deserved reward for the seventy-four-year-old grandfather with sparkling blue eyes and a prickly mustache.

Which made it all the more shocking that when James Naismith showed up for the start of the Olympic basketball competition, not only was there no special ceremony planned to recognize his presence, but there weren't any tickets for him.

After traveling 4,809 miles from Lawrence, Kansas, to Berlin, the inventor of basketball couldn't get in to watch the first Olympic basketball tournament.

Naismith's journey to Europe was made possible by his protégé and the man who had worked hardest for basketball's inclusion in the Olympic Games, Kansas coach Phog Allen. Allen convinced fellow members of the National Association of Basketball Coaches to organize a "Pennies for Naismith" campaign in the winter of 1936, with high school, collegiate, and AAU teams earmarking one cent of each ticket sold during the week of February 9–15 for Naismith's travel fund. Addressing the crowd at a high school game in Lawrence, Kansas, where fans tossed nearly $10 worth of change onto outstretched blankets, Naismith expressed his appreciation for the recognition, coming as it did nearly a half century after he invented basketball. "Don't be afraid to work for humanity," he said, "and wait for your reward." Fans stood and cheered for more than two minutes.

Apart from the donations raised at games, individuals sent in money, too, including W.A. Chain of Abilene, Kansas, who mailed a "crispy" $5 bill, and Elbert Macy of Mankato, Kansas, who parted with thirty-two cents. The McPherson Refiners sent in $9, and Gene Johnson added a dollar of his own. John McLendon earned fifty cents mowing Naismith's lawn—and handed a shiny fifty-cent piece back to Naismith. By late spring, nearly $5,000 had been collected from forty-three states, and $20 arrived from Naismith's hometown of Almonte, Ontario. The plan was for the money to be used to send both Naismith and his wife, Maude, to Europe, a "second honeymoon" for the couple, but when Maude suffered a heart attack,

*Phog Allen, left, and James Naismith, right, pose with a Kansas Jayhawks basketball player and a peach basket. While Allen and Naismith did not agree on the purpose or possibilities of basketball, Allen admired Naismith greatly and launched a fundraising campaign to pay for Naismith's trip to the Berlin Olympics. (University of Kansas Spencer Research Library)*

James sailed the Atlantic alone, leaving his wife with family in Dallas to recuperate.

Naismith toured Europe after an eight-day voyage aboard the British ocean liner RMS *Samaria*, visiting Scotland, England, Denmark, and Belgium before arriving in Berlin. Along the way, he recorded his observations in a small diary and wrote letters to Maude back in Dallas, one time purchasing a special red stamp to ensure his letter would travel across the Atlantic aboard the *Hindenburg*. He loved to stand on street corners or sit in cafés with a cup of tea and observe the goings-on, explaining that he "chose to study how people live today rather than visit cathedrals to see how they lived in the past." In his diary he noted that German women and girls were "serious," wearing no makeup and not smiling like American girls. He was surprised by the military presence on the streets, taking note of the "immense" number of different uniforms. Window displays in the shops downtown were "beautiful," and the coffee, milk, steaks, and boiled hot dogs hit the spot.

He was impressed by the energy and spirit of the white-uniformed young men and women of Berlin, though he had the wisdom to anticipate the dangers of such a coordinated effort in a dictatorship.

"Germany not only builds up its youth physically, but in the process instills in them a national spirit," he wrote. "As far as nationalism is concerned, you can't beat Germany. It may be that development in that direction can be overdone." Unlike many visitors, he saw through the façade in the city's tourist zones. "I am going to see another part of the city," he wrote, "and see the German life as it really is."

Naismith's greatest joy came in visiting the Olympic Village, where he was treated as a celebrity. Shaking off a cough he had developed on board the *Samaria*, he relished the chance to walk around the Village and chat with players and coaches from the world's basketball teams. In a letter to Maude, he wrote that he had "made a world of friends" and had his picture taken with every team. "Most of them want a picture of me standing with the coach and manager," he explained. "If I had a copy of each it would fill a volume."

*Ever since he invented basketball at an international training school in Massachusetts, James Naismith (a Canadian) considered basketball to be an international game. Here he meets a Japanese player in 1933. (University of Kansas Spencer Research Library)*

On August 7, the basketball competition began at the tennis plaza on the eastern edge of the Reichssportfeld near the Friesenhaus women's dormitory. Four of the twelve tree-lined outdoor courts had been modified to accommodate the debut of Olympic basketball, with temporary wooden backboards erected on the endlines and a layer of loam (a mix of sand, silt and clay) worked into the red clay courts to provide a harder surface supposedly impervious to rain. On each of the four courts, wooden planks surrounded the playing surface; a three-foot-high railing stood two feet back from the planks. One row of wooden bleachers lined the courts, providing seating for 112 dignitaries and media, and behind that there was standing room for another 700 spectators.

*A ticket from the first-ever day of Olympic basketball competition, August 7, 1936, in Berlin. The ticket bears the signature of Carl Diem and notes the location as the "tennisplatze." (McPherson Museum)*

Naismith showed up expecting a guest pass courtesy of the American Olympic Committee, but his name could not be found on the list. It was no oversight, but an intentional decision on the part of Avery Brundage and his staff. Naismith, they argued, had no official role with the AOC or the U.S. basketball team. Why should he receive free tickets?

This slight by American Olympic officials was compounded by the fact that the German hosts, who considered basketball a peripheral sport at best, paid no mind to Naismith, nor had they planned any sort of ceremony to welcome the game of basketball into the Olympic lineup.

For those who knew and respected Naismith, the idea that the inventor of basketball was left to stand outside the venue like a helpless beggar was intolerably embarrassing. They set out to make things right.

One such observer was Jim Tobin, an American referee working the tournament. Another was R. William Jones, the British secretary general of the International Basketball Federation (FIBA) and a former Springfield College student, who appealed for help to Carl Diem, an admirer of Naismith's.

Within a matter of hours, Naismith went from an ignored nobody to the center of international attention. Teams from participating nations hastily assembled at the German Hall of Sports, invited to carry their flags and parade past Naismith in a colorful, miniature version of the opening ceremonies. The German contingent presented Naismith with a small swastika flag, and each nation saluted the old man with a cheer, including a *"Banzai!"* from the Japanese. For Naismith, any embarrassment or disappointment he'd felt earlier in the day vanished and tears welled in his eyes. More than seventeen coaches from the various Olympic teams had studied at Springfield College; the scene felt like an international family reunion. For the first time, Naismith began to truly appreciate just what a global phenomenon his invention had become. Men from more nations were competing in basketball than any other team sport in Berlin. He addressed the crowd of two hundred.

"When I walked out on the Springfield playground with a ball in my hand and the game in my head," he proclaimed, "I never thought I'd live to see the day when it would be played in the Olympics." He congratulated the players for advancing this far and thanked them for honoring him. He later described this moment as the happiest of his life, his heart warmed by a feeling that his invention encouraged international peace and goodwill.

At four p.m., Naismith stood between players from Estonia and France and tossed one of the twenty Olympic basketballs up in the air for a ceremonial tip-off. When the sport of basketball made its Olympic debut, James Naismith was there to see it happen on an outdoor tennis court in Hitler's Germany.

The Nazis were there to see it, too. The next day's edition of *Der Angriff* ("The Attack") featured a short article encouraging people to give the mysterious new game a chance, praising the sport in ways that would have pleased both Naismith and Allen.

"Basketball is on the Olympic Games program for the first time and is still something of a 'dark art' for many of us here in Germany," the Nazi propaganda paper reported. "That's a shame, because this sport is not only good physical exercise. It's full of competitive ups and downs and always offers possibilities to captivate not just the players but spectators too."

Naismith attended each game of the tournament, befriending a German guard who helped him to his seat each day. He was delighted by the fast pace of play, thrilled by a back-and-forth game between Uruguay and Estonia, and even happier to witness countless displays of good sportsmanship. In one game, a team was left with only four players after one fouled out; the opponent convinced the referees to allow the team to reinsert another player. The fact that China and Japan even took the court against each other for a friendly game of basketball was signifi-cant, Naismith believed, given the political tensions between the two countries. At times the action was comical. Many European teams struggled with fundamental aspects of the game, with one team only passing the ball above their heads like a soccer throw-in. During another game, a player's pants fell off; he ran over toward the bench, where a teammate pulled off his own pants and handed them to his teammate, who was still standing on the court. Refereeing was inconsistent at best; some officials called traveling every time a player moved with the ball.

The rules were antiquated by American standards, with no center-court line, a jump ball after each made basket, and no ten-second rule for crossing half-court or three-second rule for standing in the free-throw lane. A player couldn't reenter the game after being substituted for except in case of injury or disqualification by fouls. The ball itself, a German "Berg" model, caused all sorts of problems. Because the leather was smooth and contained no grain, the ball was slippery and hard to handle even in dry conditions. It was also slightly oversized and, because it had laces like a football, was somewhat lopsided and difficult to dribble.

Most significant for the American team, Olympic rules only allowed seven men to suit up for a game. Coaches Needles and Johnson divided their fourteen

*The German Olympic Organizing Committee promised that outdoor courts would work well for the 1936 basketball tournament. On sunny days, the conditions were decent—even if the crowds were small.* (United States Olympic Committee)

players into two teams, one they called the Sure Passers and the other dubbed the Wild Men. Needles coached the Sure Passers, a team that included mostly Universals, while Johnson led the Wild Men, made up primarily of his McPherson players. The two teams alternated games in the Olympic tournament.

The Americans, who had been practicing at nine a.m. each day in the Olympic Village, were anxious to get started, but their opponent for their first game, Spain, never showed up. When civil war broke out in their country just as the Olympics were getting under way, Spanish athletes were summoned home. As a result, Team USA won its first-ever Olympic basketball game by forfeit. To stay sharp, the Americans played an intrasquad scrimmage and then faced their first real test against Estonia on August 9.

Art Mollner had watched the other countries practice and believed the Americans were so far ahead of their international competition they couldn't lose even if they wanted to. Still, Estonia was considered the best team in Europe and many expected them to give the U.S. team a good game. Instead, it was a rout from the beginning, with the Americans taking a 26–7 lead at halftime. Jimmy Needles and his Sure Passers had the honor of representing the U.S., and by game's end Frank Lubin led the Americans with thirteen points. Carl Shy added ten, Willard Schmidt had eight, and Sammy Balter seven. The highest scorer in the game, however, was a member of the losing Estonian team, and the circumstances making that possible caused the Americans to shake their heads in disbelief. Forward Heino Veskila simply didn't play defense, instead camping out underneath his own goal in classic "cherry picker" fashion. In a game the U.S. eventually won by the score of 52–28, Veskila scored twenty of his team's points. The Americans scored with ease by playing five men against four on offense; who cared if Veskila began most of his team's possessions wide open on the other side of the court?

An oddly organized tournament format gave the Americans a bye in the third round, meaning they had advanced to the quarterfinals of a twenty-one-team competition after taking the court just once.

Ever the flamboyant showman, Gene Johnson was forced to grin and bear it when his Wild Men had to play their August 12 game against the Philippines in makeshift uniforms; his players' red, white, and blue Spalding silks had been stolen out of their lockers the night before. Though the Filipinos were at a significant height disadvantage, with no player taller than five eleven, they gave the Americans a terrific battle in the first half, trailing just 28–20 at the break. Scribbling in his notebook, Naismith remarked that if not for the size differential, the crowd-favorite, underdog Philippine team might have won the game. But the Americans took control in the second half, dominating to such an extent defensively that the Filipinos scored just three points the entire half. Joe Fortenberry wowed the crowd in his Olympic debut, scoring twenty-one points, while Johnson's younger brother Francis added eighteen.

The semifinal game on August 13 matched the Americans against Mexico, another game the U.S. dominated from start to finish despite a pesky Mexican defense. The Sure Passers (whom Gene Johnson derisively dubbed "The Humdrums") limited the Mexicans to just two points in the first half, both coming on free throws. Leading 13–2 at halftime, the Americans coasted to a 25–10 victory, paced by ten points from Balter and nine from Lubin.

The victory meant the Wild Men from McPherson would represent the U.S. in the gold medal game, a fact that didn't sit well with the Universals. After all, they were the U.S. champions, having beaten the Refiners at Madison Square Garden. They cornered Coach Needles. *"We're your team. We're the Olympic team. This should be our game."* But there was no chance Gene Johnson was going to give up this opportunity. His Wild Men would play in the title game.

For James Naismith, the first Olympic basketball championship couldn't have worked out more perfectly, regardless of which players represented the red, white, and blue. The game would match the nation of his birth against his country of choice: Canada vs. the United States for Olympic gold.

CHAPTER TWENTY-THREE

# Strangest Game Ever

*The grounds are so well drained that even in the event of rain play can be resumed quickly after it has ceased. The International Basketball Federation has decided that the matches shall be played in the open air, and nothing will be left undone to ensure that they are carried out under conditions as ideal as if they were played under cover.* —*Olympic Games News Service, Berlin*

The puddles were so deep Sammy Balter had to pull up his pant legs so they wouldn't get drenched as he splashed his way from the locker room to the basketball courts, a three-block scamper that left him soaked to the skin anyway.

Rain had started falling the previous night, soon after the U.S. win over Mexico, and it hadn't let up since. Coach Johnson pleaded with Olympic officials to postpone the gold medal game or move it inside to the Hall of Sports, but the German organizers wouldn't be swayed. If soccer could be played in the rain, they argued, basketball could, too. The game would tip off at six p.m. as planned.

So here were the Americans, Wild Men and Sure Passers, running through the rain to the Court of Honor, a specially selected, sunken tennis court that hadn't

*Heavy rains fell during the bronze medal game between Mexico and Poland. The court turned into a soupy mess.* (United States Olympic Committee)

been used all week. Balter couldn't believe his eyes when he reached the site of the gold medal game: a low stone wall surrounded the entire playing surface, keeping all the rainwater inside. The basketball court looked more like a kiddie pool, with two inches of water sloshing around inside the walls.

Even the stubborn Olympic officials agreed the court was unplayable, moving the game to Court 4, where conditions were slightly better. With the sun hidden behind dark rain clouds, the American and Canadian players, followed by spectators emerging from underneath trees, marched through the "gloomy twilight," Balter recalled. Along the way, they passed Court 3, where the Mexican and Polish teams were playing for the bronze medal. Balter described the scene as a travesty, the consolation game taking place "in what accurately could be called a sea of mud. None of the players were recognizable, and every attempt at a dribble wound up in a [ten]-foot skid." After watching a few minutes of the game, Balter moved on to Court 4, only to find the baskets hanging crookedly from wooden backboards dripping with rainwater. So much for outdoor basketball and German engineering. "The Nazi mentality, supposedly the apotheosis of detail and organization," Balter concluded, "had misfired badly."

Truth be told, the attention of the Nazis was far from the basketball courts on this rainy evening. Instead, Adolf Hitler, Hermann Göring, and Joseph Goebbels were in the southeast Berlin suburb of Grunau, where the eight-oared rowing competition took place on a lake known as the Langer See. In 1936, crew was a far more popular Olympic sport than basketball, and the German team was expected to win gold. Instead, with millions of people around the world listening on the radio, an underdog crew of working-class American students from the University of Washington captured an improbable victory over Italy and Germany. These young men would later be immortalized as the "Boys in the Boat."

At the exact same time the American crew was making history, their University of Washington classmate Ralph Bishop huddled with his basketball teammates for one last pep talk from Coach Johnson before tip-off. Standing in the rain beside a sea of mud, the man of many words was nearly speechless. A long season that had started with a practice on October 1 at McPherson's Convention Hall would be over in a little more than an hour, win or lose. Johnson knew this would be his last game with his players. Globe executives had made it clear they would not sponsor an AAU team the next season. He had hoped to show off his fire department style of ball against the Canadians, but now it was obvious this would be no ordinary game. A fast pace would be impossible in the mud. Johnson said just three words to his Wild Men as he sent them out to the court. Francis Johnson, Carl Knowles, Ralph Bishop, Joe Fortenberry, Jack Ragland, Bill Wheatley, and Carl Shy peered through the raindrops at their coach, and this is all he told them: "Just be careful."

The wooden bleachers surrounding the court sat empty. Fans stood under trees, sat in cars parked nearby, or huddled together under umbrellas. Frank Lubin shared an umbrella with his wife, Mary Agnes, disappointed he wasn't playing, even if the conditions seemed better suited for water polo than basketball. The entire Chinese Olympic delegation was there to support Shu Hong, the Chinese referee assigned to work the gold medal game. A graduate of Springfield College who had studied basketball officiating, Shu was picked to officiate the gold medal game over the objections of some prejudiced North Americans. But Naismith "guaranteed" Shu was the right man for the job and the issue was settled.

Gene Johnson's wife, Esther, and daughter, Phyllis Lou, were there, and so, of course, was Naismith. He'd considered basketball an international sport ever since the very first game in Springfield, when boys from all over the world gave his invention a shot. He had doubted, however, that the sport would ever make it to the Olympics as long as the United States played a far more advanced brand of ball than the rest of the world. Having watched every game in the Olympic tournament, he was now convinced the IOC would eventually institute a height limit and divide into two divisions, one for tall teams and one for short. (He was wrong about the height limits, but right about the continued domination of U.S. basketball. Heading into the 2020 Olympics in Tokyo, the U.S. had an all-time Olympic men's basketball record of 138–5.)

*The first gold medal game in the history of Olympic basketball was played in a driving rainstorm. The United States, in dark uniforms, defeated Canada, in white, 19-8 in what U.S. player Sam Balter called a "hilarious travesty."* (McPherson Museum)

From the start of the gold medal game, Joe Fortenberry repeatedly provided all the evidence Naismith needed to justify his belief in a height-limit rule. Standing in the center of what reminded Fortenberry of a muddy hog pen, the world's most talented big man would win a jump ball and the U.S. team would advance down the court and score. With the rules calling for another jump ball at center court after each made basket, the pattern repeated itself. On the occasions the Canadian team secured the ball and attempted a shot, the towering Fortenberry simply stood next to the basket and, with no goal-tending rule, caught the ball as it neared the hoop.

A steady rain became a downpour. One American player had his feet slip out from underneath him as he ran down the court to collect a pass and skidded twenty feet on his behind, sending water squirting in every direction. Even in dry conditions, the Berg basketball had been difficult to handle. Now it was impossible to get a grip on it. Dribbling was pointless—the ball didn't bounce, it just plopped in the mud and stayed there. "Holding a pass," Balter said, "proved a rarity; accurate shooting, an impossibility." Watching from the sidelines, U.S. coach Jimmy Needles heard American fans gasp in disbelief as players on both teams mishandled easy passes and wildly missed shot after shot. Arthur Daley, the *New York Times* sportswriter who had been so impressed with the Refiners in New York, was dismayed to see the conditions force the Americans to play so poorly. "The game was one entirely of fumble and interception," he wrote. The U.S. led 15–4 at halftime, and the rain only became heavier in the second half. The swampy court had turned the game into a nightmare, Daley wrote, comparing the act of controlling the slick ball to handling a bar of soap in a bathtub.

Naismith despised slow play, and so did Coach Johnson, but the second half of the most significant basketball game in the forty-five-year history of the sport turned into one long, inept game of keep-away, with the Americans passing the ball back and forth just to run out the clock. As the wind grew stronger, mud and sand particles flew into the players' eyes. The ball became waterlogged and heavy, players fell and slid, and uniforms became covered in mud. At one point, Jack

Ragland became so frustrated just trying to pick up the ball, watching it slip away again and again for what felt like two minutes, he finally fell on it like a football player securing a fumble. The teams combined for just eight points in the second half, and finally, mercifully, the game was over. The United States won the first Olympic basketball championship game by the pitiful score of 19–8. Watching from the sidelines, Jimmy Needles felt one overriding sensation: he'd just witnessed the strangest basketball game ever played. Nonetheless, Canadian player Jimmy Stewart sensed he'd been part of something historic. As players from both teams walked off the court, Stewart grabbed the game ball, walked over to his wife, Mary, and placed it under her heavy blanket. "Hang on to this," he said. The ball remained in the family well into the twenty-first century. Naismith found Shu Hong, covered in mud, and wrapped him up in a bear hug, a hearty congratulations for a job well done under difficult circumstances.

Balter considered the game a "hilarious travesty" with "hardly a recognizable pivot, dribble, jump shot, fast break, or anything else resembling basketball. The Big Game had been a Big Joke." The emptiness he felt in the victory was compounded by two other nagging concerns. First, he knew he was out of a job when he got back to Los Angeles, a galling reality considering he worked for the federal government. Here he was representing the country at the Olympics and his country wouldn't even hold his job for him? Second, Balter's concern about the Nazis' true intentions for the Olympics had only grown stronger during his time in Berlin. The whole affair, he knew, had been one huge sales convention promoting the product of Nazism and its "byproducts of paganism, militarism, anti-Semitism and Fascism." Worst of all, Balter felt, most of the visitors to the Games had bought what the Nazis were selling.

Champions of the world, the Johnson brothers and their families left Berlin the next day to visit German relatives in another part of the country, missing the medal ceremony in the Olympic Stadium. Balter and the other players who did not suit up for the championship game almost missed it, too. Nobody told them when or where the ceremony would take place. Balter and Don Piper were just sitting around the Olympic Village playing cards when they decided to head over to the Olympic Stadium. There they were surprised to see some of their basketball mates on the medal stand without them. "You can imagine how we felt," Balter recalled, "when we saw the McPherson team receiving their gold medals."

As a band seated underneath the stadium's large scoreboard played "The Star-Spangled Banner" and the American flag was hoisted up the flagpole, James Naismith helped present medals to the American, Canadian, and Mexican players. No matter how much of a farce the gold medal game had proven to be, the Americans were overcome with emotion—an improbable season of victory and joy in the midst of the Great Depression leading all the way to Olympic gold. Bill Wheatley stood at the front of the American delegation and, with tears in his eyes, had the honor of receiving the first-ever Olympic basketball gold medal. His father had died in December. The Olympic experience was one of bittersweet emotion, and this moment was so overwhelming he nearly fell off the stand. Standing next to him, Joe Fortenberry swelled with pride. He cried so much he couldn't wipe all the tears away.

Naismith and other officials placed wreaths of oak leaves prepared by a Berlin

*Bill Wheatley stands at the front of the American basketball delegation to receive his gold medal. Wheatley was overcome with emotion, thinking of his achievement and the recent death of his father.* (McPherson Museum)

florist on the heads of the medalists, and each athlete was presented with a small, year-old oak sapling to plant in their hometown, a living reminder of their glory in Berlin. "This is the greatest moment of my life," Naismith said, overlooking the slapstick nature of the championship game. "I have seen basketball played at its very best."

Finally, as the ceremony ended, FIBA official William Jones noticed that one extra medal remained. He presented it to Naismith as a young girl approached with an oak leaf crown.

Those who saw Naismith later in the evening said that in the confusion and delight of the moment, he threw away his hat.

The man who arrived in Berlin with no fanfare spent his last hours in the city celebrating a colossal achievement with friends, an Olympic wreath resting atop his head.

# CHAPTER TWENTY-FOUR

# Center of the Universe

*Foreigners who know Germany only from what they have seen during this pleasant fortnight can carry home only one impression. It is that this is a nation happy and prosperous almost beyond belief; that Hitler is one of the greatest, if not the greatest, political leaders in the world today, and that the Germans themselves are a much-maligned, hospitable, wholly peaceful people who deserve the best the world can give them. On the showing of these two weeks during which all black spots have been covered, all political controversy side-tracked, all prejudice and militarism put aside and forgotten, it is all true. After the flags have been hauled down, the Olympic village vacated, the streets and hotels brought back to their normal state, and Berlin becomes itself again, one can only hope that it will remain so.*
—Frederick Birchall, New York Times, *August 16, 1936*

Before the world's Olympians returned home, the Nazis threw them one last party. On August 16, after the lights had gone out and the flame extinguished at the Olympic Stadium, there was one final, elaborate charade: the Festival of the Competitors at Deutschland Hall.

Guests drank mineral water, orange juice, and beer. They ate veal, ham, smoked pork, salami, fruit, rice, and a tomato, cucumber, and asparagus salad.

They enjoyed an array of spectacular entertainment: the Wallenda acrobats bounced off springboards and hung from ropes, ballerinas twirled, a cyclist performed tricks, and a band composed of members of a military unit known as the Leibstandarte SS Adolf Hitler provided musical interludes.

Hans von Tschammer und Osten, president of the German Olympic

Committee and Nazi sports leader, took the podium to speak. His grandiose words sounded impressive. But they were all lies.

"We know that the flame of the Olympic idea within us cannot be extinguished, for it burns as a beacon of youth," he said. "Our comradeship has been cemented under the symbol of the world-embracing five rings. It has been tested in heated and most determined contests. It will be maintained, even when we now part from each other, each going to his own country . . . This comradeship guarantees the progress of world culture, it stimulates all to competition without at the same time awakening hatred and misunderstanding. I raise my glass and think in these happy hours—in the midst of the Young Guard of Peace from all the world—of this comradeship. It shall be the guarantor for a blessed future."

The truth was that the façade that was Berlin in the first half of August 1936 was already starting to fall apart. The green garlands adorning downtown light poles were turning brown. White Olympic flags hanging along every boulevard showed spots of grime. The closing ceremonies were hardly an ode to peace, instead resembling one of the Nazis' Nuremberg rallies, complete with swastikas, cannon fire, goose-stepping soldiers, roaring chants of *"Heil Hitler"* and *"Sieg Heil,"* floodlights forming a cone of light above the stadium, and, to end it all, a stadium full of Germans singing the Nazi anthem: *"Clear the streets for the brown battalions, clear the streets for the storm division! Millions are looking upon the swastika full of hope."*

Frank Lubin remained in Berlin a few days after the ceremonies to tour with friends; he saw new anti-Semitic posters on the sides of buildings. Signs forbidding

*Even before the conclusion of the '36 Olympics, Adolf Hitler demanded his military be ready for war within four years. And while the Nazis suspended much of their public displays of anti-Semitism during the Olympics, it was common knowledge they would resume with a vengeance once Olympic visitors left Berlin. The Nuremberg rally of September 1936 shows a nation ready for war.* (Shutterstock.com)

Jewish people from entering restaurants and swimming pools that had been removed during the Games were back in their usual spots.

Before the month of August was over, Hitler assembled his aides and demanded that the army and the economy be ready for war within four years. On September 7, wealthy Jewish Germans were required to give the Nazis 25 percent of their assets, outright theft billed as a "deposit" to hedge against emigration. On September 11, the Nazis held their annual rally in Nuremberg, where Hitler railed against democracy and other speakers tried to outdo one another in their anti-Semitism. On September 25, the Gestapo arrested Jewish leaders in Berlin without any charges and Jewish pharmacists were ordered to sell their businesses to "Aryans" within a week. The post-Olympic crackdown on Jewish people, anticipated for more than a year by those willing to see the truth, was in full effect. And even as he planned for war, Hitler also imagined a new future for the Olympic Games. With Tokyo scheduled to host the Games in 1940, he intended for the Olympics to return to Germany in 1944 and remain there forever. By 1937, his architect had drawn up plans for a massive four-hundred-thousand-seat stadium in Nuremberg. This would be the center of Hitler's new world order; this is where white people would come every four years to compete. No black, brown, or Jewish athletes allowed.

African American athletes didn't need to wait for some Nazi fantasy Olympics in 1944 to experience discrimination. All they had to do was return home to the United States. When Jesse Owens arrived in New York, his wife wasn't allowed to enter some of the venues holding banquets in his honor. When the American Olympic Committee produced a book recapping the Games, a page featuring photos of gold medalists didn't include Owens, winner of a record four golds. He struggled to earn a living the rest of his life, reduced to racing against horses in minor-league ballparks just to make a buck. When Mack Robinson returned home to Pasadena, there was no celebration for the silver medalist. He could only find work sweeping streets and cleaning sewers, wearing his red, white, and blue Olympic sweater to keep warm on chilly nights. Marty Glickman, the Jewish sprinter, showed up at the New York Athletic Club to work out and was denied entry, a victim of the club's anti-Semitic policies.

When they arrived back in the States, members of the basketball team played exhibition games to finance their way back to Kansas and California. One of the games took place in Washington, DC. Sam Balter was sitting in his DC hotel room one afternoon when the phone rang; it was a woman at the front desk telling Balter he had a visitor, an old teammate from UCLA who wanted to congratulate him. Balter said to send him on up. The woman replied that she couldn't; they didn't allow Negroes past the lobby. Balter was embarrassed and humiliated as he met a gracious Ralph Bunche in the lobby. Bunche had been UCLA's valedictorian in 1927, would go on to help create the United Nations, and in 1950 would become the first African American to win the Nobel Peace Prize. John F. Kennedy would award him the Presidential Medal of Honor. But as an African American man in 1936 in the capital of the free world, he was considered by white people a lesser human.

*A celebratory Sam Balter, in dark suit second from right, and teammates arrive back in California following the Olympic Games.* (Los Angeles Public Library)

*Here's the gold medal that Tex Gibbons of the U.S. basketball team received in 1936.*
(McPherson Museum)

Balter eventually made it back to LA, but he had no job, nor did any of the other former Universals players. The Globe Refiners team was done away with, too. A marketing executive at the company was upset Gene Johnson had initially gone over his head to pitch the idea of sponsoring a team to the president of the company. As retaliation, the sponsorship was dropped. "It's a hell of a note to come back home with a world championship basketball team and have to disband it," Johnson lamented. By mid-September, Johnson accepted an AAU coaching job in Colorado Springs. His brother Francis and Willard Schmidt went with him. Joe Fortenberry and Jack Ragland joined a powerhouse team in Oklahoma. Tex Gibbons stayed in McPherson to work at the refinery. In Los Angeles, the Universals players who had not been included in the medal ceremony in Berlin watched their mailboxes, waiting for their gold medals to arrive.

Bill Wheatley returned home to Kansas a hero. A newspaper reporter asked him about his experience in Berlin. He said Germany was the most beautiful place he'd ever seen, and he marveled over how organized the Games had been. "Sometimes I think since I made this trip that we could use a 'Hitler' over here," he said. "We had the grandest trip, the swellest time possible, and it was once in a lifetime. I'd like to be starting another one like it tomorrow." But years later, Wheatley admitted he could sense danger, too. "Anyone with an ounce of brains could tell that there was a man and a country getting ready to make war," he recalled. Sprinter Anne O'Brien felt the same way, with good reason. Startled by loud noises, one night she had looked out the window of her Olympic dormitory. There in a forest under the moonlight, German troops marched in formation. She came home in August 1936 and told friends Hitler was preparing for a fight. Nobody believed her. They called her a warmonger.

Avery Brundage came back to the U.S. delivering a different message. Speaking on October 4, 1936, before a group of German Americans in New York City, many of whom belonged to pro-Nazi organizations funded by Hitler, he heaped praise on the Olympic hosts. "We can learn much from Germany," he said. "We, too, must take steps to arrest the decline of patriotism. No country since ancient Greece has displayed a more truly national public interest in the Olympic spirit in general than you find in Germany today."

In truth, Hitler was speeding the world toward war, but not before sending Germany into a massively destructive spiral of fear, hate, lies, torture, and murder. The immediate post-Olympic crackdown was followed by a series of ever more restrictive, immoral, and violent actions directed at Jewish people.

In one case, a Jewish doctor married to a Protestant woman was arrested when he was overheard joking about a Nazi song. The doctor was dragged to a torture chamber, stripped naked, savagely whipped, and urinated on by Nazi thugs as he lay dying. At the funeral, Rabbi Prinz addressed a mostly Christian audience, distraught over the direction of their country. "I am about to bury a man, a human being . . ." he said. "But if you would open the coffin, you would understand that I am not merely burying a man. I herewith bury German civilization."

An especially frightful turning point came on the night of November 9, 1938, when a highly orchestrated outbreak of violence against Jewish people took place across Germany, Austria, and parts of occupied Czechoslovakia. It was known as the Night of Broken Glass (*Kristallnacht*) because of the damage done to Jewish businesses, homes, and synagogues, with rioting members of the Nazi Party, storm troopers, and Hitler Youth burning and looting hundreds of properties and attacking Jewish people in their homes. Nearly one hundred Jewish people were killed in the violence, and tens of thousands were rounded up and trucked to concentration camps.

Even still, when Japan, at war with China, declared it could no longer host the still-years-away 1940 Winter Olympics, the International Olympic Committee awarded the Games to Germany. But on September 1, 1939, Hitler sent German tanks rolling across the Polish border, the start of what would become World War II. He had hoped to start a war within four years of the Olympics, and now his wish was coming true. By November 1939, the IOC had canceled both the Winter and Summer Olympics planned for 1940. On the morning of December 7, 1941, hundreds of Japanese fighter pilots dropped bombs on U.S. warships in Honolulu's Pearl Harbor, killing more than two thousand people, and the U.S. finally entered the war. By the time the United States dropped two atomic bombs on Japan in August 1945, more than sixty million people had been killed in the war, the vast majority of them ordinary civilians, not soldiers. Millions of Jewish people were murdered in Hitler's vast network of concentration camps, the sites of unimaginable crimes against humanity, including one million people in the Auschwitz camp alone. In these camps, men, women, children, and infants were starved, beaten, and tortured in excruciating ways. Some were buried alive; others suffocated in gas chambers or burned in ovens.

*Jewish men and boys await a train to the Auschwitz concentration camp. The Nazis murdered more than one million men, women, and children at Auschwitz.* (U.S. Holocaust Memorial Museum, courtesy of Yad Vashem)

In the lead-up to the Olympics, Hitler had declared that sporting competition unites people in mutual understanding and respect and "helps to strengthen the bonds of peace between nations." Von Tschammer und Osten had repeated similar sentiments in his speech at dinner the night of the closing ceremonies. But in Hitler's war, not only were former Olympic athletes not spared from violence and death, some were victims of extra abuse because of their Olympic histories. All the lies about peace and brotherhood the Nazis had spoken during the Olympics were exposed.

Alfred Flatow, a Jewish German gymnast who won gold in 1896, was murdered at the Theresienstadt concentration camp. German wrestler Werner Seelenbinder was beheaded. The Nazis killed Otto Herschmann at Izbica, Poland; Herschmann had medaled in both swimming and fencing and served as chair of the Austrian Olympic Committee. Two Jewish Hungarian athletes who had medaled in fencing were murdered at Mauthausen, while their teammate Attila Petschauer was tortured and died in a camp in the Ukraine. Three Dutch female gymnasts from the 1928 Olympics were captured and sent to Auschwitz, where they were murdered with their families in 1943.

French swimmer Artem Nakache competed in the 4x200 relay in Berlin in '36, where his team finished fourth. When the Nazis invaded and occupied France during World War II, Nakache and his wife and two-year-old daughter were arrested and sent to Auschwitz in 1944. The loves of his life were murdered there, but Nakache survived, tormented by guards who ordered him to swim in polluted water, to the point of exhaustion, for their enjoyment. After the war, Nakache was determined to return to the Olympics, and he did so, swimming for France in the first postwar Games in London in 1948.

Gretel Bergmann, the Jewish high jumper who had been dismissed from the German Olympic team, emigrated to the United States in 1937 and lived a long life, passing away in 2017 at the age of 103. But she remained haunted by her experience. The sight of any uniform reminded her of the Nazis and sent trembles through her body, and her sleep was interrupted for more than fifty years by a recurring nightmare. She'd imagine herself in Berlin in August 1936, standing in the middle of a swastika-drenched Olympic Stadium, with one hundred thousand Nazi storm troopers staring daggers at her. She's pulled in two directions—wanting to overcome the odds and prove a point, but also wanting to turn and run away. Over the loudspeaker comes a call for high jumpers to compete. She takes a deep breath and is ready to go, but she can't move, as if her feet are buried in cement. And at this moment she'd wake up, her body shaking, dripping in sweat.

In the war in Europe's final days, Soviet soldiers descended on Berlin. Venues that had hosted the world's finest athletes were covered in blood. Advancing Russian soldiers, allies of the Americans, won a firefight against the Germans at the site of the Olympic Village. At the Olympic Stadium where the athletes of the world had congregated in elaborate ceremonies and Jesse Owens had made history less than a decade earlier, bodies of two thousand young men now lay in the grotesque poses of death. Some German boys as young as ten years old had been ordered into service, and many were executed by their superiors here when they became frightened in battle. "The field where the Olympic youth had once assembled, the buildings and monumental grounds that had once delighted the world, had become a deadly battlefield, revealing nothing but sickening remains and gruesome debris wherever one looked," reported Carl Diem. "It struck me that not even the most fanciful poet could have imagined such a mad contradiction."

With defeat inevitable in the spring of 1945, Adolf Hitler shot himself in the head on April 30. The next day, Joseph Goebbels and his wife, Magda, poisoned their six young children to death with cyanide before committing suicide.

Germany surrendered on May 7, ending the war in Europe, and after American atomic bombs fell on Hiroshima and Nagasaki, Japan announced its surrender in 1945. World War II was finally over, and many who witnessed the carnage felt certain the world would never again tolerate such evils as racism, religious intolerance, fascism, and political persecution. If nothing else, people had learned that lesson, had they not?

But these dangerous prejudices never went away. They're still with us, and every generation must resist them. If the first casualty of Nazism was the truth, as many have written, then we must tell the truth about the past, call out dangerous lies in our own time, and raise alarms when we see justice or humanity imperiled. In his Nobel Peace Prize speech in 1986, Holocaust survivor Elie Wiesel said history has taught us that we cannot be bystanders.

"If we forget, we are guilty, we are accomplices," he said. "The world did know and remained silent. And that is why I swore never to be silent whenever and wherever human beings endure suffering and humiliation. We must take sides. Neutrality helps the oppressor, never the victim. Silence encourages the tormenter,

*The war is over! Surrounded by Hollywood stars (including Marlene Dietrich, center) Sam Balter (facing camera at left) reads news of the Japanese surrender in 1945. Balter, the only Jewish member of the U.S. Olympic basketball team in 1936, became a well-known radio announcer.* (Photo by Otto Rothschild, courtesy UCLA Library)

never the tormented. Sometimes we must interfere. When human lives are endangered, when dignity is in jeopardy, national borders and sensitivities become irrelevant. Wherever men and women are persecuted because of their race, religion, or political views, that place must—at that moment—become the center of the universe."

# CHAPTER TWENTY-FIVE

# Full Circle

October 16, 1946

*Palace of Justice*
*Nuremberg, Germany*

Outside, just past one a.m., rain fell from a cold, dark, and moonless sky. Inside, the overhead lights were uncomfortably bright, and their buzz was the only thing anyone could hear besides the sound of pen meeting paper as journalists scribbled in their notebooks, the muffled wheeze of men puffing on cigarettes, and the droning of two long ropes twitching back and forth.

The ropes were attached to a pair of black gallows that had been assembled the day before by American soldiers. On the other end of the ropes hung two Nazis, sentenced to death by an international tribunal following World War II for crimes against humanity. Neither man was dead yet, and that was the reason for the awkward silence. Guards, chaplains, judges, and journalists stood in the

*Hermann Göring, founder of the Nazi secret police (Gestapo) and commander of the German Air Force (Luftwaffe) was found guilty of crimes against humanity at the Nuremberg Trials in 1946. Here he eats breakfast in his cell as he awaits his execution. Göring committed suicide by swallowing a cyanide pill before he could be hanged by American soldiers on gallows erected on the basketball court at the Nuremberg Palace of Justice.* (U.S. Holocaust Memorial Museum, courtesy of National Archives)

uneasy quiet, waiting for Joachim von Ribbentrop and Wilhelm Keitel to be pronounced dead so that eight more Nazis could meet the same fate.

For what seemed an eternity, both men swung by their necks underneath the gallows platform. Then, at 1:30, word from a doctor: von Ribbentrop was dead. Keitel expired at 1:34. Both bodies were placed atop coffins hidden behind long black drapes. Over the next hour, the other eight men were hung. Hermann Göring's body was brought in the room, too. He had committed suicide that night by biting down on a cyanide pill he'd kept hidden in his cell.

A U.S. Army photographer climbed behind the curtains and snapped pictures of the eleven lifeless and disfigured bodies. At four a.m., the caskets were carried from the room and placed in trucks. As the sun rose, the bodies were driven to the Ostfriedhof cemetery 103 miles south in Munich.

The trucks rolled through Bavaria, the gallows were disassembled, the curtains taken down, the floor mopped. Second Lieutenant Stanley Tilles of the U.S. Army, the last man to leave the room, pulled the door closed and winced at the morning sun. "A few scuff marks on the floor," he later wrote, "were the only indication that men had paid with their lives for their participation in the most heinous regime in modern times."

This spacious chamber could now revert to its usual purpose as a gymnasium. This was the Americans' favorite spot on the property. The gallows had been brought in for the hangings only after the guards, tired and sweaty, had finished one of their regular activities.

The long black curtains hiding the eleven dead Nazis had been draped over a backboard ten feet off the ground.

Olympic basketball was born in Nazi Germany.

Nazi Germany died on a basketball court.

# Putting the Pieces Together

A few days before Halloween in 2016, I flew from Nashville to Lawrence, Kansas.

As a college basketball fan, I'd always wanted to see Allen Fieldhouse, home of the fabled Kansas Jayhawks. Also, my great-grandfather, Andrew Cummins, had been on the track team at KU in the early 1900s, where his coach was none other than James Naismith.

Those threads converged when Curtis Marsh took me on a tour of the field house and the DeBruce Center, a beautiful new building adjacent to it. Here the history not just of Kansas basketball but basketball itself came to life, with displays featuring legendary figures who got their starts at Kansas, including Adolph Rupp, Dean Smith, Wilt Chamberlain, and John McLendon. Beneath a panel of dark glass, protected like the U.S. Constitution at the National Archives, rests the original copy of Naismith's thirteen rules of basketball. A Kansas alum paid $4.3 million for the two typewritten pages, describing the rules as "the most important document in the history of sport."

As Curtis walked me past more displays, he asked a question: "Did you know James Naismith was in Berlin to see his invention become an Olympic sport?"

I'd had no idea, and I was intrigued. I had read about Jesse Owens, Louis Zamperini, and the Boys in the Boat, but I hadn't realized the Nazi Games were also the site of the first Olympic basketball tournament. I knew nothing about the first U.S. team. I did know from visiting middle schools across the country that students had a fascination with Naismith and the invention of basketball. And the Nazis. I set out to write a book about how these subjects connected.

A few months later, I flew to Kansas City and drove through the Flint Hills to tiny McPherson, where the first thing I saw was a large mural celebrating the Globe Refiners and their 1936 Olympic championship. I spent a day at the public library and the McPherson Museum, where I learned about the history of the town and the ballplayers on that legendary team. I walked into the old Convention Hall and imagined Augie San Romani's band entertaining 1,200 fans and Gene Johnson's boys speeding up and down the court, introducing the world to a new brand of basketball. Of all things, a Scholastic Book Fair was taking place on the old basketball court the day I was there. I took that as a good sign.

I learned these accomplished men came from a humble generation. They kept their gold medals and Olympic autograph collections tucked away in closets, didn't

*The town of McPherson, Kansas, still celebrates the 1936 Refiners, "1st ever Olympic basketball champions." Drive into town today and you'll be greeted by this large mural.* (McPherson Convention & Visitors Bureau)

talk much about their place in history unless asked. They got together for team reunions in 1972 and 1986, but otherwise they had no use for pomp and circumstance. Except Coach Gene Johnson. He'd talk to anybody who would listen, claiming he had "invented the modern game." There was some truth in that.

Back in Kansas City, I ate barbecue with Rich Hughes, the world's foremost expert on the Globe Refiners and that first Olympic basketball tournament. Willard Schmidt's daughter Connie Schweer showed me her father's gold medal and luggage tags from the SS *Manhattan*, and Jerry Johnson, son of Francis and nephew of Gene, told me that as a kid he used to run around the house wearing his dad's Olympic uniform. I learned that for years in McPherson, there was a doctor named Bibiano Ouano. His father had played for the Filipino basketball team that Naismith had admired so much in '36.

I studied the Los Angeles side of the story, too. I learned that Frank Lubin remained in Europe with his wife after the Olympics ended in '36 and visited his ancestral home of Lithuania, where he taught the game to eager students. Just three years later, Lithuania won the European basketball championship with Lubin serving as a player and coach. This first generation of Lithuanian basketball stars became coaches as they grew older, and the boys they taught ended up starring on the Soviet teams of the 1970s and '80s, including the 1972 Olympic team that beat the USA for the gold medal in a highly controversial game in Munich. It was the first time the U.S. ever lost an Olympic basketball game, and the first time the Olympics had returned to Germany since 1936.

*Members of the U.S. Olympic team received these luggage tags for their trip to Germany aboard the SS* Manhattan. *(McPherson Museum)*

Sam Balter, meanwhile, returned to his journalism roots, inventing a modern style of sports radio. His coast-to-coast show became extremely popular; with its mix of news and personality profiles, it was *SportsCenter* decades before ESPN came along. Until his dying day, he said competing in the Olympics was the greatest experience of his life.

I began to appreciate the most important legacy of Carl Laemmle, founder of Universal: the fact that there are thousands of people alive today who would never have existed had he not saved the lives of their ancestors. Laemmle provided the financing and affidavits necessary to help more than three hundred Jewish Germans escape the Nazis and emigrate to the U.S., including Gretel Bergmann's brother Rudolph.

It became clear that Jimmy Needles was underestimated by the Universals, who didn't think he had much talent. Needles went on to become athletic director at the University of San Francisco, where he helped build a program that became the center of the basketball universe in the mid-1950s when Bill Russell, one of the college game's first black superstars, led the Dons to back-to-back national championships, including an undefeated senior season in 1955–1956.

And remember the Long Island Blackbirds, the team that refused to play in the Olympic qualifying tournament? One of their players, Marius Russo, went on to pitch for the New York Yankees. Head coach Clair Bee enjoyed a second career as an author, writing a popular series of sports books for kids. Decades later, the Chip Hilton sportsmanship award for college athletes would be named after the title character in Bee's books. In 2010, a basketball player from the University of

New Mexico, Ramon Martinez, won the award. His grandfather had played for the bronze medal–winning Mexican national team in Berlin in 1936.

I hit the road to visit archives at the University of Illinois and at Notre Dame University, where I learned more about Avery Brundage and his AOC contemporaries. (As a college football fan, I enjoyed discovering the Notre Dame archives in the famous "Touchdown Jesus" building.) I was dismayed to see Brundage's extensive collection of anti-Semitic literature and found it revealing that even after he supported the Nazis so fervently in the prewar days, Brundage's stature in Olympic circles rose in the aftermath of Nazi atrocities: he was elected president of the IOC and held the position from 1952–1972. Perhaps this should not have been surprising. When Henri de Baillet-Latour, head of the IOC from 1925–1942, died in Brussels, Belgium, in '42, his casket was draped by two flags: Olympic and Nazi.

In Washington, DC, I visited the Holocaust Museum and the National Museum of African American History and Culture on the same day, pondering man's inhumanity to man and the strength of the human spirit. I read the profound words of Holocaust survivors and learned valuable lessons about human nature. Two themes stuck with me, opposite sides of the same coin. Elie Wiesel wrote that "those who kept silent yesterday will remain silent tomorrow." In other words, don't naïvely expect people on the wrong side of history to admit to, or atone for, their inaction or misdeeds. And in Mirjam Pressler's book on Anne Frank, she wrote that words have wings, that they endure for future generations to learn from. It requires some people to speak up—and others to listen.

I went on a bit of a James Naismith scavenger hunt. On a family road trip to

Canada, I took a detour to rural Almonte, Ontario, thirty-two miles southwest of Ottawa, where Naismith grew up. There was a statue of Naismith in the center of town and a historical marker outside his boyhood home, but what I was most excited to see was in the basement of an old wooden house by a gurgling stream in the middle of the woods. Here in the R. Tait McKenzie Memorial Museum sits the large piece of granite Naismith and his buddies used when they played Duck on a Rock, the stone that inspired basketball. Without it, there would be no fast break, no jump shot, no crossover dribble. No Kareem, no Kobe, no Steph Curry. No rusty rims nailed to red barns, no pickup games on hot city asphalt, no Nerf hoops hanging from suburban door frames. What fun would this world be without basketball? Thank you, stone!

*Tiny Almonte, Ontario, pays tribute to its favorite son, James Naismith, with a statue of the basketball inventor. Naismith's boyhood home still stands nearby.* (Shutterstock.com)

*In the basement of a museum in Almonte, Ontario, is the rock that inspired basketball, "The Naismith Stone." As a kid, James Naismith and his friends played a game called "Duck on a Rock" outside a blacksmith's shop. The object was to knock a small stone, the "duck," off this very rock.* (R. Tait McKenzie Memorial Museum, Dr. James Naismith Collection)

I learned that James Naismith and Carl Laemmle died in the fall of 1939, just as Hitler was invading Poland. But their legacies live on. As for Laemmle's, beyond the lives he saved, consider this: so much of what we think about when we think of Hollywood can be traced to an immigrant from Laupheim, Germany. He invented the concept of the movie star, created the horror film genre, promoted the first studio tour, and invited the first live studio audiences. You can visit his star on the Walk of Fame at the iconic corner of Hollywood and Vine in Los Angeles.

To learn more about the invention of basketball, I visited Springfield, Massachusetts, home of both the Basketball Hall of Fame and the school (now in a new location) where Naismith invented the game. One morning, on the way to the Springfield College archives, I stopped to admire a statue of Naismith in the Mason Square neighborhood where the old college used to stand. I took a picture, got back in my car, and ordered an Egg McMuffin in the drive-through across the street. Suddenly, it hit me. I was at the intersection of State and Sherman Streets,

*In Springfield, Massachusetts, a statue recognizes the birth of basketball in this town. At the center of the photo, one can just barely see a McDonald's at the corner of State and Sherman Streets. At this corner once stood the International YMCA Training School and Armory Hill YMCA, the birthplace of basketball.* (Andrew Maraniss)

the exact site of the old Armory Building. A McDonald's sits on the hallowed ground where the first basketball game was ever played.

On the long drive from Springfield back home to Nashville, I stopped in Cincinnati to visit the American Jewish Archives. I put on some earphones and listened to a recording from 1935, traveling back in time to hear Rabbi Stephen Wise argue eloquently against U.S. participation in the Nazi Games. On my way out the door, one of the archivists mentioned that there was a ninety-five-year-old Jewish man living in Cincinnati I might want to meet. His name was Dr. Al Miller, and he had attended the '36 Olympics as a thirteen-year-old living in Berlin.

Dr. Miller and I exchanged emails and arranged to meet at the archives a few weeks later. I was eager to learn everything I could about what it was like to be a Jewish kid in the early years of Nazi Germany. He told me about his favorite German soccer player in 1935 (Fritz Szepan), about how his parents got him out of the country in 1937, unsure if they would ever see him again. He told me how his father hid in a Berlin hospital for four weeks until the day he was able to leave Germany, evading Nazi interrogators by undergoing two unnecessary surgeries. Over the course of that month, Al's mother somehow found people who helped the Millers escape, even though the Nazis had confiscated their passports. The family reunited in Brussels, made their way to England, were detained on the Isle of Man as "enemy combatants" (because they were from Germany, even though they were fleeing the country!), and secured a loan for a trip to America. More than seventy-five years later, Miller still became choked up remembering his first glimpse of the Statue of Liberty. His arrival in America, he realized, had required a succession of miracles. When the U.S. entered World War II, Miller's fluent German came in handy. He served as an army interrogator, questioning Nazi prisoners.

In his retirement, Miller played tennis, read books, and visited schoolchildren in Cincinnati. He shared stories about the horrors of the Holocaust and the more mundane but dangerous days that preceded it, the days when he gradually lost his freedom, lost control of his own destiny, witnessed neighbor turn against neighbor.

Sometimes students asked him how we are to prevent such evil things from ever happening again, how to keep hatred and the pernicious roots of fascism from taking hold in America. The ninety-five-year-old Olympic witness and Holocaust survivor reminded them they already knew the answer. They must simply remember

*Al Miller settled in Cincinnati and, in his retirement, he met often with schoolchildren to talk about the Holocaust. He implored students to remember the final words of the Pledge of Allegiance: "liberty and justice for all."* (Andrew Maraniss)

the final words of the pledge they had recited together that very morning with hands over hearts.

Five simple words, he said, must guide their lives and their commitment to others.

"Liberty and justice for all."

*Members of the 2016 U.S. Olympic basketball team celebrate their gold medal in Rio. Heading into the 2020 Olympics in Tokyo, the U.S. team has an all-time record of 138-5 in Olympic competition. It all began in Berlin in 1936.* (Shutterstock.com)

# ALL-TIME OLYMPIC BASKETBALL RESULTS

| Year | Venue | Gold | Silver | Bronze | Team USA High Scorer |
|------|-------|------|--------|--------|----------------------|
| 1936 | Berlin | USA | Canada | Mexico | Joe Fortenberry, 14.5 |
| 1948 | London | USA | France | Brazil | Alex Groza, 11.1 |
| 1952 | Helsinki | USA | Soviet Union | Uruguay | Clyde Lovellette, 14.1 |
| 1956 | Melbourne | USA | Soviet Union | Uruguay | Bill Russell, 14.1 |
| 1960 | Rome | USA | Soviet Union | Brazil | Oscar Robertson, 17.0 |
| 1964 | Tokyo | USA | Soviet Union | Brazil | Jerry Shipp, 12.4 |
| 1968 | Mexico City | USA | Yugoslavia | Soviet Union | Spencer Haywood, 16.1 |
| 1972 | Munich | Soviet Union | USA | Cuba | Tom Henderson/ Dwight Jones, 9.2 |
| 1976 | Montreal | USA | Yugoslavia | Soviet Union | Adrian Dantley, 19.3 |
| 1980 | Moscow | Yugoslavia | Italy | Soviet Union* | |
| 1984 | Los Angeles | USA | Spain | Yugoslavia** | Michael Jordan, 17.1 |
| 1988 | Seoul | Soviet Union | Yugoslavia | USA | Dan Majerle, 14.1 |
| 1992 | Barcelona | USA | Croatia | Lithuania | Charles Barkley, 18.0 |
| 1996 | Atlanta | USA | Yugoslavia | Lithuania | David Robinson, 12.0 |
| 2000 | Sydney | USA | France | Lithuania | Vince Carter, 14.8 |
| 2004 | Athens | Argentina | Italy | USA | Allen Iverson, 13.8 |
| 2008 | Beijing | USA | Spain | Argentina | Dwyane Wade, 16.0 |
| 2012 | London | USA | Spain | Russia | Kevin Durant, 19.5 |
| 2016 | Rio de Janeiro | USA | Serbia | Spain | Kevin Durant, 19.4 |

* USA boycotted 1980 Olympics
** Soviet Union boycotted 1984 Olympics

# 1936 TEAM USA ROSTER

| Name | Height | Weight | Team | College | Birthplace |
|---|---|---|---|---|---|
| Sam Balter | 5'10" | 150 | Universal | UCLA | Detroit, MI |
| Ralph Bishop | 6'3" | 185 | Washington | Washington | Brooklyn, NY |
| Joe Fortenberry | 6'8" | 185 | Globe | West Texas State | Slidell, TX |
| Tex Gibbons | 6'1" | 175 | Globe | Southwestern (KS) | Elk City, OK |
| Francis Johnson | 5'11" | 175 | Globe | Wichita State | Hartford, KS |
| Carl Knowles | 6'2" | 165 | Universal | UCLA | San Diego, CA |
| Frank Lubin | 6'7" | 225 | Universal | UCLA | Los Angeles, CA |
| Art Mollner | 6'0" | 160 | Universal | Los Angeles CC | Saranac Lake, NY |
| Donald Piper | 5'11" | 160 | Universal | UCLA | Peoria, IL |
| Jack Ragland | 6'0" | 175 | Globe | Wichita State | Hutchinson, KS |
| Willard Schmidt | 6'9" | 190 | Globe | Creighton | Swanton, NE |
| Carl Shy | 6'0" | 170 | Universal | UCLA | Los Angeles, CA |
| Duane Swanson | 6'2" | 175 | Universal | USC | Waterman, IL |
| Bill Wheatley | 6'2" | 175 | Globe | Kansas Wesleyan | Gypsum, KS |

Head Coach: Jimmy Needles (Universal)
Assistant Coach: Gene Johnson (Globe Refiners)
Manager: Joseph Reilly (Kansas City Athletic Club)
Trainer: Eddie Zanzaai (Princeton)

# 1936 BERLIN OLYMPICS: DAY-BY-DAY

| | |
|---|---|
| August 1 | Opening ceremonies |
| August 2 | First day of Olympic competition |
| August 3 | Jesse Owens wins first gold in 100-meter |
| August 4 | Jesse Owens wins gold in long jump |
| August 5 | Jesse Owens wins gold in 200-meter; Germany's Helene Mayer wins silver medal in fencing (foil) |
| August 6 | First German pilots secretly arrive in Spain to fight for fascists in Spanish Civil War |
| August 7 | Basketball tournament begins; USA wins by forfeit over Spain |
| August 8 | Led by Glenn Morris, U.S. sweeps gold, silver, and bronze in men's decathlon |
| August 9 | Jesse Owens wins fourth gold medal in 4x100 relay; USA basketball beats Estonia 52–28 |
| August 10 | Germany loses its third straight game and is eliminated from the Olympic basketball tournament, outscored 103–43 in the three contests |
| August 11 | Future Holocaust survivor Artem Nakache and French 4x200-meter swimming relay team finish fourth |
| August 12 | U.S. women divers sweep gold, silver, and bronze medals in 3-meter competition (including thirteen-year-old Marjorie Gestring, the youngest Olympian ever to win gold up to that point); USA basketball beats Philippines 56–23; baseball exhibition game played at Olympic Stadium |
| August 13 | USA basketball beats Mexico 25–10 in semifinals |
| August 14 | USA basketball beats Canada 19–8 in gold medal game; "Boys in the Boat" win gold in eight-oared crew |
| August 15 | Italy beats Austria 2–1 for gold medal in soccer |
| August 16 | Closing ceremonies |

# ACKNOWLEDGMENTS

I'm grateful to many people for their help with this book, and I must start by thanking Bill Lacy and Curtis Marsh at the University of Kansas, without whose generosity the project never would have existed. As director of the Robert Dole Institute of Politics, Lacy invited me to Lawrence, Kansas, to discuss my book *Strong Inside*. While I was there, Curtis told me about James Naismith's trip to Berlin to see his invention become an Olympic sport. I was hooked.

The first thing I discovered in my research was Rich Hughes's important book on the Globe Refiners and their Olympic quest. Rich's labor of love, *Netting Out Basketball 1936*, was an invaluable resource, and Rich was incredibly generous to share his knowledge, advice, and connections. Anyone interested in more information on the first U.S. Olympic basketball team, as well as the Canadian team, would be wise to check out Rich's book. Brett Whitenack, curator of the McPherson Museum, was also incredibly helpful. Brett even saved the day when I lost a flash drive full of photo scans from his archives. Thanks also to the helpful staff of the McPherson Public Library.

My professional home for the last two years has been at my alma mater, Vanderbilt University, where as a visiting author I've had a chance to work alongside smart and kind people all over campus. Special thanks to Chancellor Nick Zeppos,

Dean John Geer, Wond'ry director Robert Grajewski, Dean Vanessa Beasley, Vice Chancellor and Athletics Director David Williams, and Deputy Athletic Director Candice Lee for the opportunity to work at a place that I love and for extending the flexibility to continue writing books and visiting schools. Thank you also to Vanderbilt professor of German studies Helmut Smith for his wisdom, and to Phillip McGloin, a Vandy basketball player and Luce Scholar, for invaluable research.

Anyone writing a book related to basketball would be lucky to count the great *Sports Illustrated* writer Alex Wolff as a friend and mentor, and I consider myself among the fortunate. Thank you to Alex for his support and guidance, and for providing introductions to numerous sources, including Craig Miller at USA Basketball, LIU professor Arthur Kimmel, author and Clair Bee expert Dennis Gildea, basketball historian Murry Nelson, and Jeff Monseau at Springfield College, who, along with his graduate assistant Wanjiang Zhou, provided tremendous assistance in learning about James Naismith, Luther Gulick, and the invention of basketball. Thank you also to Olympic historian and author Bill Mallon, who kindly offered to proof the text for accuracy.

Archivists are an author's best friend, and I benefited greatly from the assistance of Rebecca Grabie at the New-York Historical Society; Becky Schulte at the University of Kansas; Stephanie Klosters at the R. Tait McKenzie Memorial Museum; Jeff Pirtle at Universal Studios (thanks to Missy Davy of Creative Artists Agency for making the connection); Dana Herman, Joe Weber, and Kevin Proffitt at the American Jewish Archives; Sarah Weiss, Jodi Elowitz, and Trinity Ruggles at Center for Holocaust and Humanity; George Rugg at Notre Dame; Linda Stepp at the University of Illinois; and Ansgar Molzberger at the German Sport University in Cologne. Thank you also to Sam Balter's granddaughter Carrie Kahn for her helpful responses to numerous emails, and to Bill Bennett, Alex Timiraos, and Kat Lauer at UCLA for helping track down sources and information. Thanks also to Steve and Judy Rogers for jumping in to help with research in Amarillo, Texas, and spending a memorable afternoon with the great Oliver Fortenberry, son of Joe.

I feel fortunate to work with a group of genuine and enthusiastic people in the world of publishing, including my wise and supportive editors, Jill Santopolo and Cheryl Eissing at Philomel, who improved the manuscript in many ways and were delightful to work with; others at Philomel who helped create the book, including Janet Robbins Rosenberg, Janet Pascal, Jennifer Chung, Maria Fazio, Kristin Boyle, Deborah Kaplan, and Marinda Valenti; my agent Alec Shane at Writers House, who provided immensely helpful improvements to the flow of this book; Julie Schoerke, Marissa DeCuir, and Kendall Hinote at JKS Communications; and Steph Appell at Parnassus Books, who is not only the manager of the children's section but a student of the Holocaust. I'll always be grateful to bestselling author and all-around star Ruta Sepetys for her support and guidance; my former Philomel editor, Brian Geffen, for helping me get started in this genre; and my mentor, Ann Neely of Vanderbilt's Peabody College, for encouraging me to write for young readers. Thank you also to all the teachers and school librarians who have invited me into their schools to speak to their students over the last two years.

Writing books requires a team effort by our entire family. Thank you to my parents, David and Linda Maraniss (celebrating fifty years of marriage!), for their constant love and encouragement, and my terrific in-laws, Doug and Cathy Williams, for supporting our family in countless ways. I am extremely lucky to have two hilarious, smart, and kind young children in Eliza and Charlie, both voracious readers and writers-to-be. And to Alison, who has sacrificed so much to allow me to spend time writing books, my thanks will never be enough. I love you deeply.

# BIBLIOGRAPHY

Andrus, Burton C. *I Was the Nuremberg Jailer.* New York: Coward, 1969.

Bayer, Udo. *From Laupheim to Hollywood: The Biography of the Founder of Universal Studios.* Berlin: Hentrich & Hentrich, 2015.

Birchard, Robert S. *Early Universal City.* Mt. Pleasant, SC: Arcadia Publishing, 2009.

Bonelli, Charlotte. *Exit Berlin: How One Woman Saved Her Family from Nazi Germany.* Translated by Natascha Bodemann. New Haven, CT: Yale University Press, 2014.

Brown, Daniel James. *The Boys in the Boat: Nine Americans and Their Epic Quest for Gold at the 1936 Berlin Olympics.* New York: Viking, 2013.

Carlson, Lewis H., and John Fogarty. *Tales of Gold: Oral History of Olympians.* Chicago: Contemporary Books, 1987.

Cunningham, Carson. *American Hoops: U.S. Men's Olympic Basketball from Berlin to Beijing.* Lincoln, NE: University of Nebraska Press, 2009.

Doherty, Thomas. *Hollywood and Hitler: 1933–1939.* New York: Columbia University Press, 2013.

Draper, Deborah Riley. *Olympic Pride, American Prejudice.* DVD. 2016.

Ellsworth, Scott. *The Secret Game: A Wartime Story of Courage, Change and Basketball's Lost Triumph.* New York: Little, Brown and Company, 2015.

Flory, Raymond. *McPherson at Fifty: A Kansas Community in the 1920s.* McPherson, KS: McPherson College, 1970.

Gurock, Jeffrey S. *Judaism's Encounter with American Sports.* Bloomington, IN: Indiana University Press, 2005.

Guttman, Allen. *The Games Must Go On: Avery Brundage and the Olympic Movement.* New York: Columbia University Press, 1983.

Hamill, Pete, and George Kalinsky. *Garden of Dreams: Madison Square Garden 125 Years.* New York: Harry N. Abrams, 2004.

Hillenbrand, Laura. *Unbroken: A World War II Story of Survival, Resilience, and Redemption.* New York: Random House, 2010.

Hilmes, Oliver. *Berlin 1936: Sixteen Days in August.* Translated by Jefferson Chase. New York: Other Press, 2018.

Hughes, Rich. *Netting Out Basketball 1936: The Remarkable Story of the McPherson Refiners, the First Team to Dunk, Zone Press, and Win the Olympic Gold Medal.* Victoria, BC: Friesen Press, 2011.

Johnson, Scott Morrow. *Phog: The Most Influential Man in Basketball.* Lincoln, NE: University of Nebraska Press, 2016.

Kahn, Barbara Balter. *Sam Balter: His Life and Times.* Bloomington, IN: iUniverse, 2010.

Katz, Milton S. *Breaking Through: John McLendon, Basketball Legend and Civil Rights Pioneer.* Fayetteville, AR: University of Arkansas Press, 2010.

Lambert, Margaret Bergmann (Gretel Bergmann). *By Leaps and Bounds.* Washington, DC: United States Holocaust Museum, 2004.

Large, David Clay. *Nazi Games: The Olympics of 1936.* New York: W. W. Norton & Company, 2007.

Larson, Erik. *In the Garden of Beasts: Love, Terror, and an American Family in Hitler's Berlin.* New York: Crown, 2011.

Longerich, Peter. *Goebbels: A Biography.* Translated by Alan Bance, Jeremy Noakes, and Lesley Sharpe. New York: Random House, 2015.

Mandell, Richard. *The Nazi Olympics.* New York: Macmillan, 1971.

McPherson Convention & Visitors Bureau. *Telling Our Story: Oral Histories of McPherson.* McPherson Convention & Visitors Bureau.

*McPherson Sentinel. A Pictorial History of McPherson, Kansas.* McPherson, KS: *McPherson Sentinel,* 2007.

Naismith, James. *Basketball: Its Origin and Development.* Lincoln, NE: Bison Books, 1996.

Nelson, Murry. *The Originals: The New York Celtics Invent Modern Basketball.* Madison, WI: Popular Press, 1999.

Pressler, Mirjam. *Anne Frank: A Hidden Life.* New York: Dutton Juvenile, 2000.

Prinz, Joachim. *Joachim Prinz, Rebellious Rabbi: An Autobiography—the German and Early American Years.* Edited and introduced by Michael A. Mayer. Bloomington, IN: Indiana University Press, 2007.

Putney, Clifford. *Muscular Christianity: Manhood and Sports in Protestant America, 1880–1920.* Cambridge, MA: Harvard University Press, 2001.

Rains, Ron, with Hellen Carpenter. *James Naismith: The Man Who Invented Basketball.* Philadelphia: Temple University Press, 2009.

Rubien, Frederick W. *American Olympic Committee Report, 1936 Games of the XIth Olympiad Berlin Germany.* New York: American Olympic Committee, 1937.

Schaap, Jeremy. *Triumph: The Untold Story of Jesse Owens and Hitler's Olympics.* New York: Houghton Mifflin Harcourt, 2007.

Tilles, Stanley, with Jeffrey Denhart. *By the Neck Until Dead: The Gallows of Nuremberg.* Bedford, IN: JoNa Books, 1999.

Townsend, Tim. *Mission at Nuremberg: The American Army Chaplain and the Trial of the Nazis.* New York: William Morrow, 2014.

Ullrich, Volker. *Hitler: Ascent 1889–1939.* New York: Knopf, 2016.

Wachsmann, Nikolaus. *KL: A History of Nazi Concentration Camps.* New York: Farrar, Straus & Giroux, 2015.

Webb, Bernice Larson. *The Basketball Man: James Naismith.* Lawrence, KS: University of Kansas Press, 1973.

Whitman, James Q. *Hitler's American Model: The United States and the Making of Nazi Race Law.* Princeton, NJ: Princeton University Press, 2017.

Wiesel, Elie. *Night.* New York: Hill and Wang, 2006. Revised edition.

Wolff, Alexander. *Big Game, Small World: A Basketball Adventure.* New York: Warner Books, 2002.

*XI Olympic Games Berlin, 1936: Official Report.* Berlin, Germany: German Organizing Committee, 1937.

## JOURNALS, NEWSPAPERS, MAGAZINES

Afro-American

American Hebrew

American Israelite

Atlanta Journal Constitution

Boston Globe

Chicago Daily News

Chicago Defender

Chicago Tribune

China Press

Christian Century

Christian Science Monitor

College at Springfield Bulletin

Columbia Daily Spectator

Commonweal

Converse Basketball Yearbook 1936

Daily Mail

ESPN.com

(Toronto) Globe and Mail

Gypsum Advocate

Hartford Courant

Harvard Crimson

Jewish Advocate

Jewish Exponent

Jewish Standard

Journal of Olympic History

Journal of Sport History

University Daily Kansan

Kansas City Star

Los Angeles Times

Lubbock Avalanche-Journal

McPherson Republican

McPherson Sentinel

New Republic

Newsweek

New York Amsterdam News

New York Herald Tribune

New York Post

New York Times

Pittsburgh Courier

Slam

South China Morning Post

Sports Illustrated

St. Louis Post-Dispatch

Tablet

Time

Times of India

Triangle

Tulsa World

USA Today

Washington Evening Star

Washington Post

Waterbury Evening Democrat

Wichita Eagle-Beacon

## INTERVIEWS

Louise Allen

Mark Allen

Oliver Fortenberry

Dennis Gildea

Rich Hughes

Jerry Johnson

Jerry Jones

Nancy Kushkin

Curtis Marsh

Al Miller

Jeff Monseau

Jim Naismith

Murry Nelson

Connie Schweer

Helmut Smith

Larry Stitt

Brett Whitenack

## ARCHIVES

American Jewish Archives

Booth Family Hall of Athletics

Center for Holocaust and Humanity Education

DeBruce Center

Feldgrau.com

German Sport University Cologne

Humanities Kansas

LA84 Foundation

McPherson Museum

McPherson Public Library

Naismith Memorial Basketball Hall of Fame

National Library of Israel

National Museum of African American History and Culture

New-York Historical Society

Online Archive of California

ProQuest Historical Newspapers Archive

R. Tait McKenzie Memorial Museum

Springfield College Archives and Special Collections

United States Holocaust Memorial Museum

Universal Studios Archives & Collections

University of Illinois Archives (Avery Brundage Collection)

University of Kansas, Kenneth Spencer Research Library (Phog Allen and James Naismith Collections)

University of Kentucky, Louie B. Nunn Center for Oral History

University of Notre Dame Archives (Steers Collection)

Vanderbilt University, Jean and Alexander Heard Library

# INDEX

# Turn the page
## for a first look at
## Andrew Maraniss's next book

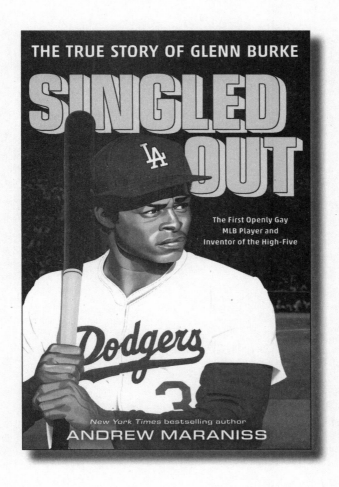

THE TRUE STORY OF GLENN BURKE

SINGLED OUT

The First Openly Gay
MLB Player and
Inventor of the High-Five

New York Times bestselling author
ANDREW MARANISS

# CHAPTER 1
# JOY AND PAIN

Bobby Haskell had learned not to be surprised by anything he encountered on the blustery streets and alleys of San Francisco's Tenderloin district.

In the early 1990s it was his job to scour these places, looking for the people most of society preferred to ignore, the drug addicts, sex workers, and runaways, the sick and the dying. As a therapist and homeless advocate for the Tom Waddell Clinic, Haskell's mission was to find these men and women, to earn their trust, and to educate them on the health care services available to them through the clinic, to offer a human connection in a world in which they felt all alone.

Haskell has never forgotten the day he walked into one of the many cheap hotels in the seedy Tenderloin in search of a homeless man his boss had asked him to track down. To call these places hotels was a stretch; they weren't national chains that offered free breakfast, a pool, and cable TV. Instead they were the kinds of dingy hostels that locked the fire escapes to keep people from skipping out on their bills. A bar of soap was a luxury. But for the men and women who could scrape together enough money (typically less than $10 a night), a room here was a step up from living on the street, even if just for a month, a week, or a day.

Haskell[1] found the room he was looking for and knocked on the door. Even by the dismal standards of the Tenderloin, this was the barest room he'd ever seen. No furniture; just a mattress in the corner. And on that mattress was a Black man, curled up in the fetal position, wearing nothing but a pair of shorts. The man was sobbing and soaked in sweat, crying tears Haskell recognized from years on the streets: tears of hopelessness, fear, and drugs.

Haskell sat cross-legged on the floor, not preaching, not judging, only offering conversation and information about his clinic's social and medical services. Gradually the man stopped crying. There was a spark in his eyes and the hint of a muscular, athletic body. In this godforsaken place, he still exuded charm and charisma.

The man on the mattress spoke with the ease of someone accustomed to meeting new people. He began to share the story of his life, telling tales of athletic feats on the playgrounds of Berkeley, California, of a professional baseball career that had carried him to the game's highest peak, of the brief but joyful days of freedom and light when he was one of the most popular men in town.

Bobby Haskell had heard all kinds of bizarre stories from people on the streets. One man had insisted that the FBI had planted radios in his thumbs; another claimed to be a Vietnam veteran suffering from PTSD, though he was far too young to have served in that war.

But Haskell was savvy enough to know the difference between lies and schizophrenia and the strange but true.

So when the man sitting across from him said he had once played for the Los Angeles Dodgers, had started in center field in Game 1 of the 1977 World Series, and had even invented the high five, Bobby believed him.

The man on the mattress?

His name was Glenn Burke.

## CHAPTER 2
# TOP OF THE HEAP

On October 11, 1977, Glenn Burke stood in the heart of the sports universe, patrolling center field at Yankee Stadium for the Los Angeles Dodgers in Game 1 of the World Series.

After spending six seasons working his way up through the Dodgers' Minor League farm system, Burke had arrived in the Bronx prepared for this moment in the spotlight.

He was an uncommonly talented athlete, even among other big leaguers, with so much potential that Dodger first-base coach Jim Gilliam had compared him to one of the game's all-time greats, Willie Mays. Dodger manager Tommy Lasorda had enough confidence in his rookie to write Burke's name in the starting lineup in the biggest game of either man's career. Teammates loved his enthusiasm and

gap-toothed grin, the laughter he brought to the locker room, the funky music blasting from his boom box.

Burke cut an imposing figure in his gray-and-blue Dodger uniform. With his broad chest, muscular legs, and seventeen-inch biceps, other players marveled at his strength and physique. He had an energy and toughness to match, never backing away from a fight. And he needed that attitude in New York. When the visiting Dodgers arrived at Yankee Stadium for a workout the day before Game 1, raucous young Yankee fans were there to greet them, rocking the team bus and shouting slurs at the players. As Game 1 unfolded, fans targeted Dodger players with rolls of toilet paper, stink bombs, whiskey bottles, and hard rubber balls.

None of this flustered Burke. Not the big city, not the Yankee–Dodger rivalry, not the stakes of the game, not the projectiles flying out of the bleachers. He had said so the day before, when he granted a sportswriter a phone interview while relaxing in his room at the Dodgers' luxurious New York hotel, the Waldorf Astoria.

"I don't get nervous no more," he confessed. "The pressure hasn't hit me yet. When everybody was grabbing and hugging and pouring champagne over my head [after the Dodgers beat the Philadelphia Phillies to advance to the World Series] I thought to myself how lucky I was to be in the big leagues . . . Everything is happening so fast. It's hard to analyze what I'm going through, but I don't want the music to stop."

The reporter asked Burke for his thoughts on playing in Yankee Stadium, a venue that was not only famous, but one of the most difficult ballparks in which to play center field. The expanse of green grass between the foul poles was enormous, with the left-center-field fence standing 430 feet from home plate, dead center 417. Just beyond the wall were reminders of the Yankees' dominant past, shrines to Hall of Famers including Babe Ruth and Lou Gehrig.

"Those monuments are real cool. I never thought anybody had stuff like that," Burke said. "Maybe they'll have one for me someday."

**But there is no monument to Glenn Burke today at any Major** League ballpark. He cherished his good fortune in life when he granted the interview on October 10, 1977, but he'd never start another World Series game after October 11. He'd be run out of baseball for good by 1980, and his life would unravel altogether a few years after that.

What happened?

To arrive at the answer, you need to know something about the Dodgers' fun-loving center fielder, a secret he kept from the public in 1977.

Glenn Burke was gay.

And as people learned this about him in the late 1970s, it was their homophobia, an irrational fear and hatred of gay people, that starved him of opportunity and launched him into a tailspin from the bright lights of the World Series to the dark alleys of the Tenderloin.

Burke died less than a year after Bobby Haskell found him on that mattress. But even in those final months, he held out hope that lessons learned from his struggles as a gay Black man in Major League Baseball would someday make life better for other people. That in his brief time on earth, forty-two years that coincided with an unprecedented period of gay liberation, he had made a lasting difference.

# CHAPTER 3
# HEART'S DESIRE

The day Alice Burke left her husband in 1952, she fixed him one last dinner.

Life had once been good for Alice and Luther Burke. He worked at the Oakland shipyards, she was a nurse's aide, and they had started a family together. Before Glenn came along, there were the four girls, Beverly, Lutha, Joyce, and Elona.

But Luther drank too much, and sometimes at night, after he closed the bedroom door, the girls could hear the commotion, fighting, and abuse. Luther had been a boxer in the navy; Alice was a sweet woman who worked hard and loved her children. She stood no chance against a drunk and violent man.

And then one day, when Alice was pregnant with Glenn, her oldest daughter, Beverly, summoned the courage to pose a question. "Why are you staying with Dad," she asked, "when he hurts you all the time?"

It was a simple question, but leaving an abuser is never easy. And for a pregnant African American mother of four in 1952 with little money and the rest of her family thousands of miles away, leaving was far more complicated than Beverly could have imagined. The next day, Alice made Luther's breakfast and made his lunch as usual. But the minute he was out the door, she started packing. When Luther came home from work that night, his wife and children were gone, and so was all but one piece of furniture. Alice had left Luther dinner on the kitchen table.

She took the kids to Louisiana to stay with her parents for a few months, saved some money, and proved a point to Luther: she would not tolerate his abuse. She and the girls ultimately moved back in with Luther in Oakland, and Glenn was born there on November 16, 1952. Alice's strength and courage revealed Luther's weakness; he wanted nothing to do with a family he couldn't control through fear. By the time Glenn was eleven months old, Luther moved out. Though he occasionally came back to visit, he eventually started a new life with a new family, far away in Alaska.

**With or without their father, this was a family that was emblematic** of the East Bay in the mid-twentieth century. During World War II, thousands of Black sharecroppers moved to Oakland from the Deep South to build ships. By the war's end, the city's African American population had quadrupled. But after the war, the shipbuilding and other manufacturing jobs disappeared. With jobs scarce, more affluent white residents left town—one hundred thousand of them between 1950 and 1960 alone. The people left behind faced mounting economic and social pressures: fewer jobs, freeway construction and urban renewal projects that decimated businesses and neighborhoods, and eroding city services. And when Black citizens called for justice, the response from the white establishment was to tighten its grip. Poor Southern whites who had also moved to the Bay Area for wartime jobs were recruited to join the police force. They brought their racial attitudes with them from Dixie, and often used their state-sanctioned power to abuse Black citizens.

It was in the midst of this tension that Alice Burke raised her family, moving between homes in North Oakland and South Berkeley. Berkeley, home of the University of California, was emerging as its own hotbed of conflict in the 1960s as administrators cracked down on student protests against the war in Vietnam and racism at home. For a young Glenn Burke, the political and social changes in Oakland and Berkeley (the "East Bay" across from San Francisco) were not yet much of a concern. He felt the strength and love of his mother, the protection of his older sisters, and the friendship of a mix of Black, white, Asian, and Latinx friends on the block. The home was constantly filled with people: the sisters and their schoolmates, their boyfriends, and extended family. Alice loved to cook, and the smells from the kitchen were a reminder of her Louisiana roots: gumbo, yams, mac and cheese, potato salad—all made from scratch.

Glenn was a "pretty good kid for a boy," his sister Lutha recalled, and even when he did get into trouble, it was "usually something laughable," she said. He and his buddies would stand on the street and break into applause whenever a car drove by. The driver would look around and wonder what was happening, and while Lutha could never understand the appeal, Glenn and his friends got the biggest kick out of it. Other times, they'd jump out of the bushes and throw water balloons at passersby, hiding just in time not to be seen (or so they thought).

If this was a home mostly filled with love and laughter, there was one occasional interruption: Luther's infrequent visits. Alice and her ex remained on speaking terms, and sometimes he'd come by the house. Lutha wanted nothing to do with her father. One time he showed up on the doorstep, suitcase in his hand and coat on his arm. She slammed the door in his face and said dryly to her mom, "Your husband is on the porch."

The drop-in dad would attempt to "toughen up" the boy who lived with all these women, picking on Glenn, roughhousing with too much force. Just trying to make the boy hard like him, he'd say. As much as Luther's visits made Glenn anxious and uncomfortable, he still found pockets of peace: at the playground, in church, drawing pictures, listening to music, singing. He had a beautiful voice. And it was that voice that led to one of two formative experiences in the life of a young Glenn Burke, his first taste of the spotlight.

In December of 1961, just after his ninth birthday, a white folk-music trio known as the Limeliters announced they were looking for talented schoolchildren to sing along with them as they recorded a live album. Glenn, then a student at Lincoln Elementary, was one of fifty Berkeley kids handpicked to participate in two live concerts recorded for the album. Dressed in a gold sweater, Glenn joined a multiracial group of children singing along with the professionals, belting out tunes such as "Lollipop Tree," "Stay on the Sunny Side," and "America the Beautiful."

The album appeared in stores early the next year. *Through Children's Eyes: Little-Folk Songs for Adults*, sold for $4.98 and was a hit with reviewers. "Kids Steal the Show" read a headline in Des Moines, Iowa. Years later, Lutha said the experience provided Glenn a window to a larger world. "He grinned the whole time. It was just a wonderful opportunity for him to connect with kids and adults of all races," she said. "At that time, there were not many opportunities for something like that. It probably set the tone for his life."

**Around the same time, Glenn experienced another glimpse of fame.** On Saturday mornings, he and his sisters loved to watch *The King Norman Show*, a local children's television program. With his wife and French poodle as sidekicks, host Norman Rosenberg donned a royal gown (actually his bathrobe) and jeweled crown and turned the television studio into a magical world known as Happy Bedlam, which he ruled with "kindness and gifts." Recorded in front of a live studio audience of children and moms, the show was, according to one newspaper description, "a pasteboard empire of popcorn and candy, toys and talent." The program featured pogo stick races, guessing games, and talent shows, and there was one segment designed to make even the most sugar-high kid sit at attention, perhaps even shed a tear. Each week, a child who had written a heartwarming letter asking for a present for themselves or a friend was invited to sit in the Heart's Desire booth.

Glenn's oldest sister, Beverly, decided to write a letter to King Norman. She was shocked to receive a phone call from the television station with the news that her letter had been selected. So the next Saturday, Beverly dressed up and everyone went down to the studio. The time came for the segment, and Beverly took her place in the booth. King Norman read her letter out loud. "All the little boys in the neighborhood like to ride their bikes, but my mom can't afford to buy Glenn one. My heart's desire is that Glenn could have his own bike so he can play with the other boys in the neighborhood."

As the studio audience cheered with delight, King Norman asked Glenn to come down to the stage, where he presented him with a brand-new red bicycle.

"What are you going to do for your sister to thank her for writing in?" Norman asked.

"I'm going to let her ride the bike when we get home," Glenn replied.

But that promise didn't last.

"He wouldn't let nobody ride that bike," Lutha recalled decades later. "We'd ask him, 'What about what you said when you were at the TV station?' He'd just look at us and grin."

As far as young Glenn Burke was concerned, he had now starred on television and recorded a live album. He knew what it felt like to stand apart from the crowd. And there was one other way in which he felt special back then, an aspect of his being that would come to define his self-worth, for better or worse, for the rest of his life.

At his core, Glenn Burke was an athlete—one of the best anyone had ever seen.